W9-BLF-507

Light AND Leaven

Most Reverend Bishop
Joseph E. Strickland

Light AND Leaven

THE CHALLENGE OF THE LAITY IN
THE TWENTY-FIRST CENTURY

Catholic
Answers
Press

Published by Catholic Answers, Inc.

2020 Gillespie Way

El Cajon, California 92020

1-888-291-8000 orders

619-387-0042 fax

catholic.com

Printed in the United States of America

Cover and interior by Russell Graphic Design

978-1-68357-183-4

978-1-68357-184-1 Kindle

978-1-68357-185-8 ePub

To my flock in the Diocese of Tyler

CONTENTS

FOREWORD

By the early years of the twenty-first century it was clear that the Catholic Church had been afflicted with bad bishops.

Some were bad men, without question. They stole money. They lived decadently. They partied and engaged in loose sexual lives. And they abused others in ways that suggest they could not possibly have believed in the God of the Gospels.

Many more were good men who were just bad at being bishops. This may be because they misunderstood their moment. A new model for the modern office of bishop was needed because entirely new challenges had emerged, but these bishops were, in far too many cases, corporate men, allergic to innovation or bold action.

They might have made fine professors or pastors had they never been elevated to the office of bishop, but, having been elevated, they failed.

They failed to act as spiritual fathers to their own priests. They failed as administrators. In the face of a worldwide revolution in morals, they failed to teach right and wrong as it had been taught since the time of the apostles. They allowed the liturgy to be trivialized. They allowed every kind of compromise with the world to infect the institutions in their charge.

And they apparently thought they were doing a good job, because they kept teaching—as if the thing that the world needed was more documents from them.

The sheer volume of written instruction composed by the Catholic bishops of the world in the last two decades of the twentieth century is almost beyond comprehension. Millions of words poured out, primarily published through state and national bishops' conferences. Most of these documents were given scripturish-sounding titles, as if the bishops were handing them down from angelic realms. Here are just a few titles from the U.S. bishops in the eighties and nineties:

Strangers No Longer
A Place at the Table
Welcoming the Stranger Among Us
A Commitment to All Generations
Living the Gospel of Life
Called to Global Solidarity
A Catholic Framework for Economic Life
Sowing Weapons of War
The Cries of the Poor Are Still with Us
Communities of Salt and Light
The Harvest of Justice Is Sown in Peace
A Matter of the Heart
Renewing the Earth
Called to Compassion and Responsibility
Economic Justice for All
The Challenge of Peace

Certainly, the content of some of these documents was fine. A few even made a positive difference in their time. But most of this material was, and remains, ignored.

The lack of self-awareness evident in this wordiness can hardly be exaggerated. While the Church drifted into its greatest crisis in 500 years, the world's Catholic bishops formed committees, gathered for meetings, and year after year promulgated new rounds of new documents.

Then, in 2002, the *Boston Globe* dug around a little and found a lot being covered up in the Archdiocese of Boston. Something shattered. Catholics had begun what George Weigel later called the "Long Lent."

News stories gushed forth in 2002, 2003, 2004, 2005 . . . until there remained hardly a Catholic alive who did not ask wearily, "What kind of an institution am I involved in?"

All of this recent history means that any man made a bishop now has no excuse for conducting business as usual.

If, after all that has happened, he goes back to running his diocese like a business, if he cuts corners as a moral teacher, if he lets the institutions within his diocese make corrupt compromises, and if he relies on bishops' conferences to do the job of teaching for which he, as a successor to the apostles, is supposed to take personal responsibility, he will not be just another beleaguered modern bishop; he will be a fully culpable failure.

One of the electrifying signs of life in the Catholic Church of the 2020s is the number of bishops who seem to get this; who seem to grasp the gravity of their moment. A few are even trying their hand, little by little, at apostolic boldness.

These are the post-trauma bishops. Whatever else they do, they are determined not to fall into the traps that led to the Long Lent.

A leader has emerged among these post-trauma bishops out on the plains of East Texas. Bishop Joseph Strickland of Tyler, a diocese of about 100,000 Catholics scattered over thirty-some rural counties, has taken creative pastoral and educational initiatives within his diocese, has used social media to address the wider Catholic community, and has sometimes challenged other bishops in public forums—all with an unrehearsed frankness that has roused lay Catholics.

It might seem dismissive to say it, but what inspires many is Bishop Strickland's style more than his substance.

This is not an insult, however. Not at all. Most of the bishops who led the Church into disaster were, in fact, quite solid on the substance of Catholic teaching. They simply lacked a style of leadership that communicated the substance of the Faith as what it is—the most important thing in the world.

In 2018, at the USCCB's annual conference, Bishop Strickland asked his fellow shepherds a simple question that electrified Catholic social media: "Do we believe the doctrine of the Church or not?" The video of his question went Catholic-viral for a simple reason: the lay faithful want this kind of talk. They want to hear bishops talking to each other in this way. They take it as a sign of health.

In the not-too-distant past a bishop from a place such as Tyler would almost certainly have blended into the background, and quite intentionally. He would have refrained from making hard comments at bishops' meetings or challenging the actions of the national conference of bishops. Whatever pastoral actions he took would have conformed to the consensus. In plain language, he would have gone with the flow.

That Bishop Strickland is not following those old rules is what has won him a wide and appreciative audience. That he comes from a tiny and unglamorous diocese is not held against him but taken as a mark of authenticity. The laity are sick to death of the affected decorum of the pre-trauma years. They want no more of the pecking orders their leaders seem, all too often, to cherish.

They want bishops who *bishop*.

The salient point about a bishop is not the size of his diocese, the public figures he's photographed with, or any other consideration except this: he is a successor to the apostles of Jesus Christ. The laity are thrilled at any sign that these men remember this and take it seriously.

In some ways it is too easy to criticize the bishops of the late twentieth century.

Just as the sexual revolution was tearing civilization apart, the Church was living through the period of confusion that followed the Second Vatican Council, and quite suddenly, these bishops were no longer leading robust Catholic communities. They were presiding instead over a Church that had become as fragile as an earthquake-damaged high rise.

They were not fools to tread carefully. The whole thing really was in danger of collapse. The compromises they made were not in every case the folly of weak men. They were sometimes the prudent efforts of men swamped by new realities.

Consider the example of Catholic universities, which in the seventies and eighties became dissociated from the core mission of the Church and, in practice, became places where Catholic faith and tradition were denigrated.

We might well fault the bishops for their many failures to stand up to the administrators and faculties who were setting Catholic young people at odds with the Church. But in the general confusion of those times, it still seemed possible that the universities might reform themselves, which would have meant the bishops did not need to further divide and scandalize the faithful by waging battles against what many of the laity still took to be trustworthy Catholic institutions.

Everywhere, good Catholics—normal, everyday Catholics—were presented with confusion and rebellion. It was all mixed in with genuine reform and honest attempts at renewal.

Was it really such a bad thing for a bishop of those years to try to hold things together in the hope that some kind of normalcy would soon return?

In a sense, the bishops of today have been liberated from that species of hope that was holding the Church back: hope that the calamity threatened by the many rebellions raging within the institutions of the Church might be avoided if they just waited it out.

That hope failed; the calamity came anyway; and what did the Church get for all its efforts at pacification? The way forward now is obvious: purification by clarity.

Bishops must live and teach the Faith with clarity so that others can make an informed choice. Does this Catholic school want Catholic doctrine or not? Does this Catholic hospital want Catholic doctrine or not? And this marriage? This lay leader? This priest?

This is the choice of our moment: whether to be Catholic in the fullest sense or to let that option fade, for the foreseeable future, into darkness.

To present this choice with stark clarity to both individuals and institutions is, today, a mercy. It permits others to come to their own decisive moments. It frees everyone from the pretense that a comfortable accommodation can be made with a world in revolt against reality.

Of course, clarity will have costs. It will lead, almost certainly, to a loss of money, a loss of opportunities to cooperate with government, a loss of public prestige, and a loss of comfort.

But clarity will also produce something of incalculable value for our entire confused and shattered late-modern world: a choice.

If the Church clearly and fearlessly offers just what Jesus and the apostles offered, the world will have a truly humane alternative to its current anomie. And unless they are given this choice, billions will live and die without ever receiving a serious invitation to become sons and daughters of the living God.

Here is the secret about the Church right now: the laity are ready to be challenged. They have gone through the Long Lent. They see the world growing dark. And while the Church has been in her crisis, they have been building new institutions: new Catholic universities, Catholic media networks, joyfully Christ-centered lay movements.

What they need now are leaders.

It might well not have been true in the seventies, eighties, or nineties, or even in the early years of this century, but it is true now: if good bishops will step forward and lead, they will find a laity equipped and ready to follow. They will find new institutions at their disposal. They will find boldness in the pews—brothers and sisters ready to stay with the Church whatever comes.

Because he speaks plainly, many will quibble with this or that position of the bishop of Tyler. He seems incapable of speaking in the mollifying generalities of a corporate man. But whatever arguments you might have, I can assure you that in the following pages you will meet a bishop who knows his moment, who understands that God's people are ready for the challenge, and who is doing his East Texas best not to let them down.

—Cy Kellett
  Host, *Catholic Answers Live*

INVOCATION

Almighty God, your Son has conquered death and risen from the dead; guide us by the strength and the power of his resurrected light.

His death and resurrection brought the leaven of the Holy Spirit into the world; help us to know your wisdom and to seek always your Holy Spirit.

May the blessed Virgin Mary intercede for the bride of her Son, the holy Catholic Church, and for each of us as disciples today, that we may be faithful and strong in following His light.

We ask this in the name of your Son, Christ our Lord.

I

Light

First-Century Christians in
a Modern World

People lament that there is no longer a Christendom, but, you know, Christendom wasn't exactly heaven on Earth. The Church doesn't have worldly power any longer, and I don't think that's a bad thing.

So it has to be nuanced, this idea that we're living in a post-Christian world that's so much worse than it was in the past. In some ways, we're more similar to Christians living in the Roman Empire of the first century than to those in other eras throughout the centuries. It's almost like we're starting over, in the face of intense opposition, with the original mission of the Church: to bring the message of Jesus Christ to every corner of the Earth.

This means that the Church, her guiding light, her leadership through the hierarchy, is more needed than it has been in many centuries. The world is not just post-Christian; it's post-God. There's an angry resistance to truth and authority. If there is no God, then there is no authority, and no one can tell me what to do. That's how we operate now. Moral anarchy. There's a whole tone in the press, in government, in universities—even Catholic ones—saying we need to throw off this mantle of oppression.

In their atheistic or post-theistic worldview, people view as oppression any impingement on what they falsely believe to be their freedom. Religion, God's agency, is viewed not as liberating and enlightening but as oppressive and controlling. And the Catholic Church is still seen as the big gorilla of religion, so she gets to be the biggest target of people's rage against God and against authority.

The idea that human beings are made [or created] male or female is oppressive because it doesn't let people make humanity whatever they want it to be. Marriage as a natural institution ordered to one man and one woman for life oppresses people's wish to form sexual partnerships with whatever person or persons they choose—or end them at will. It's oppressive not to let people kill babies in the womb because we all should be allowed to define human life for ourselves.

None of this is real freedom. That's hogwash. It's an ugly and sinister conception of freedom that is ultimately slavery to the self.

The Challenge of Anti-Humanism

THUS, ANTI-THEISM'S ULTIMATE end seems to be anti-humanism, a sense that human nature and human beings are the problem in the world. We see this in the rhetoric of some environmental activists and even some of the unfortunate preparatory materials for the Amazon synod, suggesting that humanity is like a virus on the planet, that this could be a wonderful and pristine planet if it weren't for *people*.

What occurs to me is that in the Easter vigil, the Genesis reading talks about how, at the beginning, there was a formless wasteland. Then God in his creative activity, which flows from his love, began to give form to that formless wasteland. So there is no perfect natural world without God. We take him out of the equation, and there's just a wasteland. And when God's gone, human beings are just little individual formless wastelands with no image, all on our own in a meaningless moral void. It's such a bankrupt, ugly view of life that it really surprises me how far people can take it.

Sadly, even within the Church some have lost a lot of commonsense humanism: that robust sense that we're made by God with a nature (male and female, created in God's image) that is good, though wounded, and ordered toward certain ends.

But I don't see how people can be on that track and continue to live, continue to have any sort of perspective on life that gives meaning to getting up in the morning. If you're on that track, it's hard to find meaning, much less hope, in your life. And that's tragic, because there is meaning and hope in the world. Christ isn't dead. He rose from the dead, he is alive, and he offers us his life. He's the light of the world, and he wants us to bear that light.

If we reject God, we will never truly understand ourselves. This is embedded in divine revelation:

God has revealed to us that we are created in his image and likeness. If we leave him out of the picture, then we have nothing to measure ourselves against. Full, authentic humanism means recognizing that we have both natural and supernatural life—something our supposedly enlightened world ignores. Rekindling that humanism, renewing in the world that full view of mankind and our heavenly destiny, is the laity's great challenge in our age.

Rise and Shine

IF YOU WANTED to, I think you could go back to the Protestant Reformation to find the roots of our current cultural challenges. But in my lifetime—I'm a Baby Boomer, born in 1958—we seem to have gotten on an accelerated pace of moral corruption and denial of God. There has always been sin, of course. But in our age, we seem to think we're God. We think we're in charge, that we're in control, and that is the root issue.

We see parallels between our time and the ancient world into which Christ came. In the Roman Empire, the Caesars thought they were gods. There was abortion and infanticide. There was awful sexual debauchery. Look at the brokenness of the Roman Empire and fast-forward twenty centuries to where we are now, and it's the same brokenness, and it comes down to the same denial of God and of his sovereignty over us.

The darkness that we face is deep; it has been building for centuries, permitted by God for whatever reasons. It seems like we're reaching a crescendo of evil. But, remember the old ditty, "Better to light one candle than to curse the darkness"? I think we need to be candle lighters. We need to be torch lighters, *bonfire* lighters of the light of Christ in this darkness. I think we have to acknowledge the darkness and acknowledge that Satan and evil are powerful, but Christ has overcome them.

"Do we believe in Christ or not?" Sometimes our Church does not give a resounding forceful, joyful, powerful *yes* to that question. I, personally, have been too shy about boldly proclaiming this wondrous deposit of faith that we have in the Catholic Church. But if we truly believe in the Easter mysteries, how can we be silent? We have to be witnesses to the risen Lord.

We need to wake up. To what? The truth of the octave of Easter. This truth that the Son of God suffered, died, and rose for all humanity. And it's not just a nice story. It is a world-changing reality, and we have to help people understand that.

Evangelical Protestants talk a lot about Jesus as their personal Lord and Savior. I've always tried to emphasize that as Catholics we need to embrace all of that as well as recognize that we have blessings in the sacraments, in the Real

Presence of Christ in the Eucharist, in this vast deposit of faith, the teachings of the Church, the *Catechism*, the lives of the saints. The treasures of the Church are endless, and we have to hold fast to those treasures and share those treasures.

When I was ordained a bishop, I wanted not just a pectoral cross but a crucifix, because at this time I believe we need *Christ* on that cross: body and blood, soul and divinity, that flesh that suffered and rose. We need to focus on that image, front and center. We need to be very clear about who we are and who God is: that is the way out of this corruption.

The Durable Reality of our Faith

IF THE CATHOLIC Church isn't about supernatural faith, what is it? It began at the Annunciation when an angel told a young woman, a virgin in Nazareth, that she would be the mother of the Son of God.

And we believe that at that moment, when she said yes, the Holy Spirit conceived in her womb Jesus Christ, who is God's divine Son, who had existed from all eternity. If that's not radical supernatural faith, I don't know what is! We have to build from there to really be the Church, yet a lot of that has gotten lost. We smirk at some mysteries instead of believing them with our whole heart.

So, do we believe these things or not? I believe them. I believe that the angel Gabriel spoke to Mary and this really happened; it's not just a nice story or a symbolic reimagining of more mundane events. Neither are these revealed, supernatural manifestations of God's love, power, and judgment just our version of some universal fairy tale. It's not, *I like Hansel and Gretel and you like Goldilocks, and somebody else likes the Three Bears.* No, it's not myth. It's not just nice stories. It's hard reality.

As a Catholic community we have to decide whether we really, radically believe in these supernatural mysteries or not. I do. I believe they're more real than this desk I'm sitting at and all the other material things I'm surrounded with. If they're not, we might as well just close the doors of St. Peter's and turn off the lights.

The Role of a Bishop

BEING A BISHOP is a tremendous challenge: to truly shepherd the people of God as a successor to the apostles, to bear the apostolic zeal of the first-century Christians, to grow ever deeper in relationship with Jesus Christ. Our last three popes—John Paul II, continued with Benedict XVI, and now Francis—have emphasized that personal relationship with Jesus.

In November, it will be eight years that I've been bishop, and I thank God for giving me lots of opportunities to develop the realistic humility that every priest needs, but especially a bishop.

Especially in this time, I think to be a humble servant is one of the necessary hallmarks of a bishop.

That humility also includes the key element of seeking the truth and knowing that the Church is the Lord's Church, not mine. My office has been the same since the time of Peter and James and John and Andrew, all the original apostles, including the betrayer, Judas Iscariot. Just as with the original twelve, today's episcopacy involves men encountering the great mystery of Jesus Christ and called not just to encounter him (as every Christian is) but to be coworkers with him in a privileged way.

In the Mass readings from Acts during the octave of Easter, we hear stories of those who saw Jesus, walked with Jesus, related to him personally after the Resurrection. Like the apostles after Pentecost, we bishops have received the Spirit, the grace of our office. I have felt it, and people have seen it. It is a grace of humility before the person of the Lord whom we serve.

It's good for me, as a bishop, to have my feet on the ground, to be aware that I'm just a man. I'm a sinner. I have gifts, but I certainly have deficits in my life, as we all do. I'm not strong enough sometimes. I'm not smart enough sometimes. But if I keep my feet on the ground, I know the Lord will use me.

My diocese is heavily non-Catholic, and many of the Evangelical Protestants and others in this community would say, "No, thank you," to us as Catholic pastors. *We don't need you, we don't want you.* But evangelization is our mission. Those non-Catholics are people of God, too. And I think that that's one of the basic themes of my work as bishop: to constantly remind myself and others that the Catholic Church is not a group or a club for the elite few. We believe this is truth, for all humanity for all time. It's not just our little Catholic thing. It's for the entire world. And that's a pretty bold vision, but it's the vision of the Church.

Jesus Christ, by the will of the Father, came into the world to save humanity, not to save just a certain nation or people. At the time that Christ was walking the earth in the area of Palestine, the apostles didn't know about the area where I am sitting now, here in northeast Texas. They didn't know that most of the people and places in the world even existed. But they knew they had to bring Christ to all the world. And I think that's a powerful reminder to us in the twenty-first century. We have a global call, a global call of individual church communities. This call to be the voice of truth for all applies to me in my little see of Tyler, and it applies in all places where the Church is (or should be) a dominant force in society. I am blessed to have wonderful priests who are truly dedicated to that mission: the mission of this one local church to be fully the Church.

St. Ignatius of Antioch said, "When you have a bishop, a priest, and a deacon, there is the Church." And so I am in charge of this little corner of the Church, just as the bishop of Rome is, just like the archbishops of New York, Los Angeles, Sydney, Rio, Paris. If people were sitting down to list the great dioceses of the world, they wouldn't even know Tyler existed, much less put it on the list, but in spiritual terms, I have exactly the same mission and the same responsibility as bishops of great dioceses.

That sort of blows you away. I can't just coast here. I can't just maintain. I have to be a successor of the apostles, witnessing Christ's truth to the world he put me in, just as they did. St. John the Baptist points to Christ and says, "He must increase, and I must decrease." If I'm doing the work of a successor of the apostles, I have to say the same. I have to increase the presence of Christ and fade into the background myself.

Back to the Fundamentals

PEOPLE DON'T TRUST bishops now. I was going into a supermarket here in East Texas, and just walking in the door, a man looked at me dressed as a bishop with the zucchetto on and all of this— sort of a startling sight, I have to acknowledge that. But he said, "Well, here walks in the most corrupt institution in the history of humanity."

It isn't true, but the corruption has diminished our stature among Catholics and in the general population, and sadly, that diminishes the power of our teaching and witness, the teaching and witness meant to save souls.

The Church has become too much of the world. When I first became a bishop, the model that I saw and that I began to adopt was that of a business manager. The model that I received was *find these programs, watch the money, get some great staff, be a good delegator, and, oh yeah, pray.* Instead, it needs to be pray, pray, pray, and then the management will . . . not take care of itself, since we need to use our God-given talents to make wise choices financially and all those things. But it has to be driven by prayer, and honestly, that was not how I started out as a bishop.

I was really far from what the real call of a bishop is. But more and more, I have felt called to pray first— to pray *reverently* the eucharistic liturgy first—and then the rest will flow out of that. It's about my conversion first. It's about me being faithful to Jesus Christ. I still have a lot of growth to do, but God's grace has been working on me since I was ordained a bishop.

Some of my fellow bishops are brilliant, some are above average, some are just nice guys, some are very strong, some are very clear, some aren't clear at all. It's a mixed bag, a variety of human gifts and human deficits. And there are many good men becoming bishops, but the model that the Church is offering to a newly ordained bishop now is not the healthiest. We need to go back into the centuries, to look at bishops of the past and popes and how the Church addressed challenges through sanctity and prayer. That's how we will bring the light of Christ to the world.

In sports, coaches talk about going back to the fundamentals. If your team isn't doing well in football, or baseball, or basketball, go back to the fundamentals. How do you dribble? How do you throw a pass? How do you block and tackle? I think we bishops have to go back to the fundamentals as Christians and as Catholics, and be strong in them, and teach our people to be strong in them.

The World Needs a Strong Church

I THINK THAT a lot of what's wrong in the world is that the Church is so weakened and so corrupted that she's not that beacon on the hill, not leaven for the world, any longer. She can be leaven, and she hasn't lost the light, but the corruption is deep. Yet I do not blame the Second Vatican Council for that. I blame the human corruption that was already there prior to the council. As a kid who grew up in the sixties and seventies, I remember so much of that in the larger culture: the turmoil, the lack of respect for authority. It seemed like the whole world cried, "Who has the right to tell me anything?"

Well, the Church has not just the right but the responsibility to share the truth that Jesus Christ offered with his own body and blood; but when the Church falters, the world shakes. And that's what we've seen and are seeing. The fabric of human civilization is dependent on the Church's playing her role, the most significant role, more significant than any nation or any other power on Earth. Because it's not our power; it's the power of the Son of God over everything in heaven and on Earth.

And if we really believe that, then the Church has to deal with this corruption not just for her own sake but for everyone's sake; so human beings can flourish in this world and have everlasting life in the next. I said something like that at the USCCB that probably got some smirks. But the very last canon of the *Code of Canon Law* says all of this is ultimately about the salvation of souls, and that's the mission of the Church. That is the everlasting life we're called to, but when the Church is as corrupt and beleaguered as she is today, then the world's in trouble.

The Smoke of Satan in the Church

I WAS AMONG the very last of the U.S. bishops chosen by Pope Benedict, only a few months before he resigned.

Pope Benedict's resignation was one of those moments like 9/11, like Kennedy's assassination.

I remember exactly where I was standing, who told me. I was getting ready for a Mass here at the Chapel of Sts. Peter & Paul, just a regular morning Mass. I remember standing there and this deacon I'd worked with for years tells me that Pope Benedict is resigning. I thought, *What? Popes don't resign. This has to be fake news.* But, of course, it wasn't.

I remember watching on television as the helicopter flew from St. Peter's and took Pope Benedict. For those first few days, he went off to Castel Gandolfo, and then . . . okay, where does a resigned pope go?

At that moment, the ground began to shake under me as a bishop. It's been shaky ground ever since.

A lot of ink has been spilled trying to figure out what really was motivating Pope Benedict. I don't claim to have the answer, but based on what he has said, I guess he didn't think he had the strength to reform the corruption in the Church. And now Pope Francis is dealing with a corrupt monster that I don't think any individual could really tackle, honestly. But he has brought some strength, and by the grace of God, all things are possible.

Certainly, it's *only* the grace of God, the power of the Holy Spirit, that will cleanse this corruption in the Church and in the world.

Our January *ad limina* visit was a very pleasant gathering, but somewhat disheartening to me because it was almost too pleasant. Things weren't pleasant, from what I could see, in the life of the Church. There was too much confusion, too many people wondering about disruptive and confusing things like the Amazon synod, too many Catholics not clearly and joyfully proclaiming the truth of Jesus Christ as the apostles did back in the first century.

I asked about the McCarrick report, and we got

something of an answer, but we still haven't seen it.

But of course, there's lots of information out there about some really scandalous things that have gone on, whether financial or sexual impropriety or whatever it is. The corruption always seems to go back to the same areas: sex, money, or power. And a lot of times, it's all three woven together, as with the sad legacy of McCarrick. His ability to raise money brought him power, and power let him abuse people sexually and get away with it. He was too much of the world.

You can't be a McCarrick and really believe in the Church's call to the priestly ministry, so whether it's insanity or evil I use his name to signify the kind of corruption he exemplifies.

Then there are many less dramatic cases of priests who just struggle to live up to their priestly commitments as fully as they should; priest with substance abuse issues, or emotional issues, or relationship issues that aren't sexual but are still inappropriate for a priest who should be chaste in all he does.

That's a challenge for men in the world today and certainly for priests. As a bishop I try to be a father to them. They are my spiritual sons. I must pray for them and especially with them. I must be quick to share an encouraging word and remember to express congratulations and appreciation for a job well done. (As with all fathers, it's all too easy for me to get caught up in my work and speak up only if there is a deficiency.) I think it's also important for a bishop to take the time to get to know his priests as men; what are their favorite things, their interests, their hobbies? It's always enriching to me personally and to the bond I have with my spiritual sons when I learn something of the men that is outside the usual ecclesiastical world.

I don't have all the answers, but I try to be guided by the love of Christ, leading my priests in the call away from sin—to integrity, to purity, to dedication. Thankfully, in Tyler we've had minimal issues with abuse or other such scandals, though we've had some vestiges that had to be dealt with—always with the understanding that we can be renewed in God's mercy.

Yet we must also be sober about the times that we live in; we have to recognize the reality of evil. As Pope Paul VI said, the smoke of Satan had entered the Church. I think that we're seeing that smoke become at times a roaring fire. Evil is real, and evil is powerful, but the Son of God died and rose and conquered the power of evil.

And so we have to be joyful and we have to have faith. As Christ said, "The gates of hell will not prevail." Now, we tend to think of this as a guarantee. "We've got God on our side, no matter what." It's true, but it can also lead to complacency. Christ and the Church will prevail, but the Church may get battered. She may lose souls. She may suffer greatly. The Church could soon look very different on the outside.

Christ didn't give us any guarantees about that. Let us not take his promises and be complacent, as if there were no work for us to do, no battle for us to fight. We must continually defend the Church from outside attacks and reform the Church's corruption from within.

The Laity's Role after Vatican II

ALL OF US are called to holiness. At times in the Church there has been a tendency—never explicit, but a tendency—to leave the holiness to the holy people—that is, the ordained or the vowed religious. If you look at the beginnings of the Church, that wasn't the case at all. Everyone was called to discipleship. But at times, the Church fell into habits of thinking otherwise.

I think the Second Vatican Council was trying to reinvigorate some of that broader understanding of holiness and discipleship. And that is the number-one challenge the laity face today: making the Catholic faith *a way of life*. Not something you do for an hour on Sundays, leaving the rest to the clergy, but a way of living your days. An all-encompassing approach to the human journey.

It sounds so countercultural, yet the council was not inventing a new thing or asking the laity to do something they had never done. It was restoring the call to holiness as a universal call for all the baptized.

There's a lot of debate over Vatican II—with many people saying that it put the Church off track, that the Holy Spirit couldn't have guided it, and some even saying that it wasn't a true council. I simply don't believe that. In the years that followed, the Church (and the world) did get off track. But if you read the documents of Vatican II, and I constantly return to them, they express beautiful truths that are universal and timeless for all humanity. The smoke of Satan did enter the Church, and it corrupted the implementation of the council. It diminished reverence for the Mass; it confused Catholic teaching on faith and morals; it emboldened enemies of the truth inside and outside the Church. But neither the council's aims nor its documents are the reason for this corruption.

The reason was not Vatican II but the "spirit of Vatican II." I grew up with the idea, and when I went off to the seminary in 1977, about a decade after the council, that "spirit" was powerful. But the spirit of Vatican II was not the Holy Spirit. It was a human spirit. It was a spirit of compromise, a spirit of dilution, a spirit of weakness and surrender.

But the antidote to that spirit is not to go back and erase all of the letter—to throw away the '62

Missal, to act like the council didn't happen. I do believe that we need to get back on track, but to do that by reading and actually following what the council documents say. Not reading them with eyes informed by the insidious, worldly "spirit of Vatican II," but with eyes of faith, of continuity with the tradition of the Church. The council was meant to be an enrichment of the tradition, a re-presentation of it, not a total departure from what came before

Beauty and Confusion in the Papacy

WHEN POPE FRANCIS was elected and first started speaking up, I remember people here in very Evangelical-Protestant, non-Catholic East Texas stopping me in the parking lot and saying, "Isn't our new pope great?" They were impressed with what they heard, the emphasis on remembering the poor, and the simplicity that Francis seemed to be bringing to the papacy. There are some beautiful elements there: going beyond the church walls and going out and accompanying people. There's much beauty in what Pope Francis has brought to the papacy.

But along with him have come some troubling reports that have been unsettling for people who really believe in the Catholic faith, and even for a bishop sometimes it's hard to know what's fake and what's real. (I wouldn't want the job of Pope Francis or any pope in this time. It's tough enough to be a bishop of my little diocese.) The beauty that Pope Francis brings to the papacy comes with a shadow of confusion, and sometimes it's hard to reconcile those two.

Pray for Pope Francis. He is the Roman pontiff, the vicar of Christ in the world today. He's got a job that is beyond any of us to accomplish without the supernatural grace that the Church offers.

Liturgy at the Heart of the Church

THE LITURGY IS at the very heart of the Church. It's at the very heart of personal renewal and conversion to a deeper faith, and it should be at the heart of every individual's journey in the Lord. In the liturgy we welcome the King into our own lives personally. The pinnacle of the Mass is the bread and wine becoming the body and blood, soul and divinity of the Son of God, and then he's there to nurture us. The greatest connection we have with our Lord Jesus Christ is through the eucharistic liturgy, where he becomes really present to feed us, to strengthen us, to help us avoid temptation and sin, and to bring us the joy of being an alleluia people, not just during the Easter Octave, but always.

This also means that renewal in the Church as a whole must begin with Jesus Christ on the altar in the liturgy.

Certainly, the bishop is the chief liturgist for the diocese, so he should set a tone and be a model by how he celebrates the liturgy. But the bishop can't hover over every Mass that's celebrated. That would be a broken approach even if somehow it could be made possible. Yes, bishops need to set the model, and I'm very conscious of that. But the daily responsibility lies with the priests. They should teach their parishioners to have reverence for the Holy Eucharist, really impress upon them that the celebration of the Mass is a moment when we kneel before the Lord of the universe. Priests should explain the parts of the Mass, the teachings of the Church, and the moral precepts of a Christian life in addition to all their very important pastoral duties.

Paying attention to the smallest detail is loving Christ. If the liturgy tells us to use these words and only these words, I think we need to pay attention to that. I think all of us—priests, deacons, bishops, laity, everyone who approaches the altar—need to develop that mindset.

It wasn't always my mindset. I've done some things that I will never do again, back when the Church was wandering through a lot of those weeds. I used to gather the people into the sanctuary around the altar. I don't do that anymore—it's the wrong focus for what are we doing. When I was a young priest, I used to let students bring up their sports equipment during the offertory procession in Masses at the school cafeteria. Why did I think that was appropriate?

And I remember singing one song—and music so often reveals how we are approaching the liturgy—that I actually liked, I confess, but the theology was bad. It was called "God and Man at Table Are Sat Down." It was the whole "communal meal" approach, very cozy. Oh, isn't it nice? We're having a meal with God.

Of course, the liturgy is rich with levels of meaning, and there is a sacred-banquet aspect to it, but this is secondary to, and a result of, the sacrificial aspect. But the sacrificial part so often gets left literally off the table. The wonder of the banquet aspect is that by it, we receive the sacrament by which Christ feeds us spiritually with the *body that he sacrificed for us*. So emphasizing the meal first is missing the point; it's only a banquet because first the sacrificial victim was slain for the sins of the world.

We must also remember that it's *God's liturgy*. We are its humble servants, bringing the people at the eucharistic altar to encounter the Lord as he offers himself to the Father. The Roman Missal, then, is more than a how-to manual for pulling off a ceremony; it's a *spirituality*. It's a whole organized effort to use human means to place us before the divine.

A due concern for reverence doesn't mean that every layman needs to enlist in the liturgy police and write to me every time Father doesn't hold his hands exactly as he's supposed to. (And of course, unfortunately there are people who like it when a priest freelances during Mass.) That some people feel it necessary to patrol every Mass for irregularities, though, only underscores how important it is for priests to submit to the Church and say the Mass exactly as the Missal lays it out, no more and no less.

That's another argument for *ad orientem*: it really helps to take the priest out of center stage. I use that term intentionally because sometimes the sanctuary is treated as a stage, a place to perform and entertain, rather than a place of sacrifice. In that place, the focus must not be on the priest. That's totally wrong. The priest—and the people with him—should be focused on Christ. The body language of *ad orientem* helps reinforce that focus, and it reduces the opportunity for the celebrant to ad-lib and thereby shift the focus to himself.

The architecture and layout of churches play a part in this as well. So many of the churches built in my lifetime—and the way they are configured—are just wrong. We've all seen, I'm sure, many different aberrations that make you stop and ask, "Who did this and why?" It's just bad theology played out in wood and stone: seemingly designed with a conscious aversion to beauty and set up to direct our attention to anywhere but Christ on the altar. The presider's chair placed smack-dab in front of the altar, for instance, telegraphing that the liturgy is about him.

In contrast, we speak of liturgical architecture being *theocentric*: having "God at the center." The classic cruciform church literally places God at the center and through the ages has proven conducive to liturgy that lifts us to God. The altar must be prominent and make a statement that leaves no doubt that it is at the heart of the building. The tabernacle should be clearly linked to the altar with an ebb and flow between the reserved presence of Christ and the immediate presence as bread and wine once again become his body and blood at the Mass being celebrated.

Too many churches require a map to find the tabernacle! Instead there should be a natural flow from reverence for Christ present in the tabernacle as the faithful gather for Mass, to a focus on the wondrous moment when he comes anew on the altar with the words of consecration, to those who receive him, and finally back to a reverence for his reserved presence in the tabernacle as the Mass ends and the congregation is dismissed. The architecture of the liturgical space should lend itself to this natural flow with reverence for our presence in the house of the Lord always at the forefront. The building where the altar of the sacrifice of Jesus Christ is located should be like no other, and it should say in every way possible: *God is here; this is his dwelling place.*

Show me where the elements of the liturgy—music, architecture, postures, fidelity to the Missal—direct your focus, and I'll tell you whether you have a liturgy that is reverent and God-centered. And then you'll also know whether you have a liturgy that is spiritually fruitful for the people.

Christ Always Front and Center

PERSONAL DEVOTIONS ARE an essential part of Catholic spirituality. The rosary, for example, is very important to me. But the rosary is not the totality of everything, and neither is any other individual prayer or pious practice. The laity need to be on guard against a mentality that says, "Everything has to be the rosary," or "Everything has to be Divine Mercy," or "Everyone needs to go to confession weekly and the priest should just live in the confessional because confession is so beautiful" (which it is). Instead, we must constantly ask ourselves, "How does this bring us to Christ?" He is where we're all headed.

Mary wants us to focus on her Son, the Son of God, Jesus Christ. So yes, the rosary; but how do we use it along with a lot of other things to draw us closer to Christ? People's pet projects can't be the totality of their spiritual lives, which must be centered first on Christ in the Eucharist in the liturgy.

The same goes for different ministries and programs that a parish has. Sometimes people will contact me and say, "Bishop, we've got to reach out better to our youth." *Absolutely,* I say. But the Church can't just become the Youth Project. That would be as out of whack as any other primary focus that is not our eucharistic Lord.

How do we bring our youth closer to Christ? Programs and social events and special catechesis can all be useful. But the answer begins with the liturgy: proclaiming through our communal worship the person of Jesus and his saving sacrifice. He's there, he's really there, in the Mass. Any outreach to the youth that doesn't begin and end with this central truth is doomed to failure.

And so all of these things, every devotion, every sacramental, every ministry, everything we promote needs to bring us to Christ. And the liturgy is the most proximate way we can encounter him and encounter him more and more deeply.

On Liturgy Wars

THE LITURGY IS the principal source of strength for the individual Christian, strength for families, strength for parishes, strength for dioceses that are local churches in the world, and strength for the universal Church. It all flows from Christ, and the liturgy is our closest connection to him. It's tragic, then, that so many essential elements of the beauty of our Catholic faith have been caught up in the Liturgy Wars. There's such division over liturgical preferences and liturgical ideas; we fight over the sacred elements of the liturgy like children with toys. It's a tremendous scandal.

Instead of squabbling, we have to be patient with each other and try to focus together on the principal thing that matters: reverence and keeping that focus on Christ always. The more we can purify our approach to the liturgy in this way, the more we can grow in respect for every form of liturgy that brings us to Jesus.

That includes what's called the *Extraordinary Form* now, the traditional Latin Mass. The more I learn about it, the more I offer Mass in this form, the more I see what Pope Benedict was trying to do with *Summorum Pontificum*. This form of the liturgy shouldn't be thrown into the trash bin. It should be something that continues to be part of the living life of the Church.

But neither do I think that what's called the Ordinary Form just needs to go away, that we should just erase everything after the 1962 Missal. I truly do not believe that.

We're there to worship God. We're there to focus on the theocentric. We owe God worship—that's a basic revelation to the people of Israel. The Holy Mass is the liturgy of liturgies, the most perfect way to fulfill this duty here on Earth. We have it because Jesus Christ poured everything out to worship the Father, to complete the will of the Father, that his own Son would be sacrificed in order to make it possible for his earthly children to one day dwell with him. The Mass re-presents that perfect worship of Christ.

So let's not dwell on what kind of liturgy "speaks to me more" or "helps me approach the sacred." These are the wrong questions.

Are we worshiping God in reverence or not? *That* needs to be the question.

Loving the Liturgy in All Its Forms

LATELY I'VE GROWN in my own personal under-standing of and spiritual incorporation of what the liturgy really is about. And I feel like I'm just getting started (don't we all?). If we believe in what the Mass is; if we say, "Yes, this is some-thing literally I will die for," then the next step is to ask what kind of liturgy brings us to that final gift of the real presence of Christ.

After the Protestant Reformation, we know that the Council of Trent said, "Okay, we're going to sort of lock things down. *This* is the Catholic way." It was necessary, but it tended to suppress the richness of liturgical expression. There are many different rites in the Catholic Church. In the seminary, I didn't learn anything about them. Later, I learned a little bit as I stud-ied Canon Law and the Oriental Code.

And then, since I've been a bishop, I've gone to some of the liturgies of the various Eastern churches that are in union with Rome, that are part of the Catholic Church. And I've been struck by their beauty and reverence. Yet they don't even figure into the Latin-vs.-vernacular debate. They're just different, equally beautiful and rich historical examples of how we pray formally to accompany the re-presentation of Calvary.

They do contrast quite a bit with the post-conciliar liturgy especially. In the period after Vatican II, perhaps influenced by American culture, we got off-track liturgically by wanting things too quick, too simple, too straightforward. Even when I was born, in 1958, there was a lot of Americanization of what was still the Latin Mass, what we call the Extraordinary Form. The low Mass was culturally moving us toward what the Ordinary Form is now: a simplified, get-it-done approach that is very American. We believe, but we want to do it quickly because we have other things to do.

If you look at some of the divine liturgies of the Oriental rites, *simple* and *straightforward* are not in their vocabulary! They are complex, mysterious, fulsome. This is fitting, considering that in them we approach the greatest supernatural reality we can encounter in this world.

That we have more than twenty rites in which to experience this reality also seems fitting: a rich and varied set of ways to celebrate the loving sacrifice of Jesus Christ, the Son of God, and to receive the fruit of that sacrifice that he has offered us to sustain us, to give us our daily bread, his own body and blood. Rather than throw out or suppress any of these liturgies, I think the Church needs to embrace and enrich our understanding of each of them, to help us see the elements that are all authentic, different ways of celebrating and coming to the pinnacle of the liturgy, which is always that the bread and wine become Him.

And yes, that includes broadening and deepening our understanding of the Extraordinary Form and making it more widely celebrated. Yes, it can be daunting for people at first—even for me, as I'm just learning to offer it. It's in Latin, and there's all this stuff, and the priest is dressed funny, and it looks as if it's all in secret. It doesn't seem as clear or as straightforward as the Ordinary Form. "It's just too much going on there. . . . Give me the Ordinary Form—you can map it out very easily without learning an ancient language."

It seems to me that the Ordinary Form is like the simple melody line of the song, whereas the Extraordinary Form is like the full-blown symphonic presentation with the woodwinds and the horns and the percussion and the strings and everything, harmonies and melodies interwoven. Visually, the Ordinary Form's music sheet is one simple line of notes, whereas the Extraordinary Form sheet is so packed with notes that at times they blur together. The Ordinary Form is sparser and more linear: do this only and then move on to the next thing. In the Extraordinary Form it is more complex, and a lot of things are happening all at once.

One of the aspects that I truly appreciate about the Extraordinary Form is that every note speaks of Jesus Christ. I believe the Ordinary Form can do exactly the same thing, but it is up to the individual praying to fill in the blank spaces with notes of Jesus. In the Extraordinary Form, my impression is of all the blanks already being filled in, leaving your energy directed toward allowing each note to truly resonate Jesus in your prayer.

And of course, the Extraordinary Form is less prone to the irreverence that detracts from the respect for Christ and the spirit of sacrificial worship that is proper to the Mass. It's less likely to overemphasize human community building, or the horizontal dimension of liturgy, at the expense of its rightful focus on God. You find this, for example, in some modern hymns that don't even mention God at all!

So I think we must remember that the end point, the pinnacle of the liturgy, is Christ himself. Not just remembering him, not just listening to his words, but celebrating his real presence. He shows up; the King of Kings shows up at Mass every time it's celebrated validly. If we keep that focus, then whether we get to that encounter with the Lord in Spanish or English, or in a combination, or in Latin and English, or in French and Latin—all of that is just the human form of getting us there—then we're doing liturgy right.

And then, okay, how do you dress for this? How do you prepare yourself for this? What kind of music do we want to use? What sort of elements do we want to bring to this? If everything is through the lens of the presence of

God's divine Son, of his coming to dwell with us on the altar, then we don't want to meet him in a raggedy tee-shirt and gym shorts. Neither do we want to greet him singing some sappy tune that somebody just wrote on a napkin.

Instead, let's bring our very best to the King of the universe: to celebrate him, to worship the Father . . . and to be transformed ourselves. For the liturgy lifts us to the divine. It reminds us of what our destiny is.

Entering the Mystery More Deeply

LET US STAY hungry for the Lord. Our hunger, our need for him, is why he has given us the eucharist rites. He instituted the Eucharist at the Last Supper because he knew that we needed food that would sustain us, just as the people of Israel needed food in the desert. We're in the desert of a culture that doesn't believe in the supernatural. In order to pass through that wilderness, we need to be fed by Jesus daily. He wants to feed us. And his food will be most fruitful and sustaining when we receive him with proper reverence and disposition of heart.

That's where we have to start. We have to believe fully and unreservedly in the mystery before us. We must prepare ourselves through confession and penance. We try to be as worthy as we can of receiving him.

I certainly wouldn't claim that, in the Diocese of Tyler, every liturgy is pristine and theocentric and wonderfully focused, and the music is great, and all the people are saints. That's just not reality. You can't flip a switch and have everything fall into place at once. But I believe that if we are focused on who and what we're receiving and how to be rightfully disposed, then we are going to dress differently. We're going to bear ourselves differently. We're going to appreciate the silence that allows us to take into our hearts and minds what is actually happening.

Believe me, here in East Texas I've had people say, "Oh, bishop, please don't make us do Latin. We don't understand it." They think Vatican II did away with Latin forever. But the Vatican II documents on the liturgy actually say that Latin should be preserved.[1] The express intention was never to totally dispense with Latin in the liturgy but to mix in the vernacular with it. The two can coexist.

I've been studying what's now called the Extraordinary Form of the Mass, the Latin Mass, and I have been learning things that I never knew about the liturgy. (I was in a good seminary, considered one of the more stable, more orthodox and conservative seminaries in the Church in the late 1970s, but the Extraordinary Form was never

---

1   *Sacrosanctum Concilium* 36.

offered to us as something that we should study.)

As I pray before the Blessed Sacrament, I've been inspired to do a lot of things differently, and the main thing I'm after with the liturgy is reverence, because of the real presence of Jesus Christ. We believe that Jesus Christ, body and blood, soul and divinity, is truly there. And a lot of that real faith, that something that enlivens us and guides us through life, has been lost.

The low Mass of the Extraordinary Form has a lot of quiet built into it. The Roman Missal in the Ordinary Form says we should pause for some silent prayer. Yet, as a culture, we're scared to death of silence. We rush to fill every moment and every place with music, talk, some kind of noise. Without good catechesis and good explanation, intentional silence in the liturgy can lead to people just sitting or kneeling there without entering into a deeper relationship with the Lord. Just a couple of minutes would seem like an eternity. "Is Father all right?" "Did he fall asleep?" "Did he forget something?" Rather than using the time fruitfully, they get preoccupied with those thoughts the whole time until the silence is over.

Silence is something that our culture struggles with, but I think it's necessary in the liturgy, to give some breathing room to the supernatural things we're celebrating. The liturgy needs space and time to let it soak in.

Ad Orientem, Ad Deum

SOME CATHOLICS WANT a return to receiving Communion at the altar rail so they can receive on their knees. Others say that's "reactionary," pre–Vatican II, a step backward to something we've moved past. I hear both comments a lot.

As always, the key to evaluating these things is reverence. If altar rails are something that will increase reverence toward the Mass and the

Eucharist, then that's a step forward, not backward. Or we might need a reform of the sign of peace, which shouldn't be a hootenanny but a simple greeting of those immediately next to you. I think the nod and smile that many parishes have been doing because of social distancing may turn out to be a good practice that we hang on to.

We should look at the most reverent ways we can approach receiving the body of Christ and indeed every element of the liturgy. And that could include offering Mass *ad orientem* more widely. I appreciate how it is physically theocentric: the priest and the people together facing the Lord. *Ad orientem,* as you know, really means facing the *east*, with churches traditionally built with that orientation toward the east, toward the rising sun.

But I think *ad Deum* is an even better term than *ad orientem,* because it's about turning to the Father as Christ does. He turns to the Father and gives his life in sacrifice of love for all humanity. That's what we're celebrating. To be turned toward the Father as Christ is turned toward the Father: it makes a lot of sense.

There are places, even in the Roman Missal now, where it explicitly says, "Facing the people, priest does X." And I've had younger priests arguing, "See, it even says . . ." So it's *almost* there—not explicitly, but almost presuming that you're *not* facing the people at other times; almost like a remnant of the original intention. Perhaps this is part of why Cardinal Sarah has been such a proponent of celebrating Mass *ad orientem*. I do think it's worth looking at more closely.

I have to say, since I have started studying liturgy more closely, learning about the Extraordinary Form and trying to emphasize reverence in my diocese, I know that I celebrate Mass differently. I may be facing the people, but I'm not looking at the people the way

I was. I'm looking more at the Missal, looking more toward Christ—trying to gaze at the presence of Christ on the altar. I think people can pick up even those subtle things that the priest is doing, creating a greater atmosphere of reverence and awareness for those who are there.

Even someone who knows nothing about what the Catholic Church believes, even an alien from Mars, if he is intelligent, should be able to pick up on the priest's focus and what that signifies. For many decades now in so many parishes, though, I don't think that such a stranger would have picked up on what the Mass means. He probably would have said, "Well, this is just a gathering of people. Something happens on that big table up there, but it doesn't seem to be the real focus." Our goal for reverent liturgy should be for a stranger to come in and immediately say, "I'm not exactly sure what they're doing, but something really important is happening on that altar."

I would love for that to be how everyone sees me and every priest celebrating the Mass. *The important thing is happening on that altar—I can tell by their focus.* The Extraordinary Form makes it harder to avoid that impression, to change that focus, and so it's instructive for the way we celebrate the Ordinary Form, too. We must be focused on worshiping almighty God first, not just being a happy little community together—which is great, but it's not the liturgy.

People are hungry for the transcendent, for the divine. They're hungry for something that calms the restlessness of their hearts, which, as St. Augustine said, are restless until they rest in God. That speaks to our basic existence as human beings. That restlessness takes all kinds of different forms, and some of them affect people in a way they can't express or quite put their finger on. Maybe they aren't even very aware of what is troubling their hearts.

But good liturgy must speak to that longing, to that restlessness that nothing in the world can quell. There are all kinds of gatherings of human beings, but what we should do in our Catholic churches should leave no doubt that we are encountering the divine—that we are making present the answer to their troubles, the fulfilment of their restless hearts' desires.

That's just the way God has made us. Just as children tend to gravitate toward what's authentic and what's real, we all desire something real to grasp onto. *This is something real for me.* That child is still in each of us; those supernatural answers to the meaning of life are available to us in the Holy Mass.

How to Fix Catechesis

I'm one of the products of decades of intentional watering down of catechesis. The *Baltimore Catechism* was laughed at—just a lot of silly

memorization. (Though I think people are redis-
covering now that there is a lot of wisdom in
memorizing some things, to make them part of
who you are.) It was all thrown out, caught in a
wave of catechetical and educational theories that
appeared in the sixties and that the Church rashly
adopted. "Just make the children feel cozy and
embraced and warm, and they'll sort of soak up
the truth later," the idea went.

It didn't work. And it led to a spirit of relativism that made all ideas, all acts, all lifestyles
equal to each other. There was no longer real
truth or real sin. In that case, why stay Catholic?

Many catechists were volunteers just trying
to do their best, of course. They had faith and
they wanted to teach, but the materials and the
mandate they were given were vacuous. They
weren't instructed or in some cases allowed to
say anything meaty about the Faith. And you
would be surprised how much even young

children can understand without dumbing down. Certainly, you use language that's appropriate to their level of education—no ten-syllable words—but even with basic language you can communicate, and have them grasp, very significant theological truth.

But beginning with my generation this was largely abandoned. So a lot of people left the Church, because however warm or comfortable or loved they may have been made to feel in their CCD classes, that alone couldn't sustain them. They needed to wrap their minds around the truths of the Faith and be brought face-to-face with its deepest mysteries. This didn't happen, and so they walked away.

It's a tragedy that, as bishop, I see more clearly than ever that people are walking away from their faith without every really knowing it.

This is why I have declared my intention for the Diocese of Tyler to be a teaching diocese. And that we have to see teaching as *formation*. Catechesis does require learning and memorizing some things, but it doesn't stop there. We're not just disembodied brains; we're incarnate beings. Religious education is a whole-person undertaking.

This means we must relate catechesis to real human experience. I like to remind people that the seven sacraments all deal with natural aspects of being human: we all get hungry, we all get hurt, we all need to say we are sorry, we all need a direction for our lives, and so on. Catechesis also needs to take into account other "accidents" of people's lives. If you are ill, the gospel takes on a different meaning. If you are scared, it takes on a different meaning again. The gospel should meet people where they are; adapted (but not diluted) to teach and edify people according to their life circumstances. Christ offers us the perfect model: he encountered real individuals where they were, and he brought them his light.

We have all the human needs, and certainly that is how we have to approach teaching. And that is a work in progress as well. As the Church, we're always thinking in eternal terms. We should be in the long game—a marathon, not a sprint.

Faithful Parishes = Good Catechesis

IT'S VERY PROPER for people primarily to live out and be taught their faith in the context of their *parish*. It's part of subsidiarity, a basic and Catholic principle of organizing human civilization— and one that we really need to bring back and breathe new life into!

We start with the individual man or woman getting his or her life ordered in the way of Christ, and then in the household. Then, for most people, the parish is where the households, the families, come together to support each other. Now, is the catechesis that occurs, whether directly, in classroom religious education or in homilies, or indirectly, in the life and witness of the parish, strong enough to counteract the secular catechesis that we're all immersed in? Not by itself, but it's a necessary beginning. The parish can be the foundation that supports people as they take the truth of the gospel out into the world.

But, even leaving aside the disruption of parish life during the pandemic, too many Catholics would say they're on the rolls at a parish, but that's about it. They go to Mass on Sunday, but their parish isn't a center of their way of life. To be truly catechetical, to truly form Catholics as whole persons who will be light and leaven for the world, parishes need to become places where the Way of living Jesus Christ fully in the Catholic tradition is supported and nurtured, and made joyful, and imaginative, and creative.

How does a pastor accomplish this on his own? He doesn't. It has to be delegated; and the more you delegate, the harder it becomes to achieve that kind of catechesis that successfully plants the truth that will counteract the tidal wave of false messages that comes in the culture. That is more than an uphill battle for any parish, especially the very large ones. So a big part of the challenge we face is to be united in purpose in our Catholic communities—starting with what we believe. Yet our belief is often so fractured.

I think we talk a lot, and especially in the very Evangelical Protestant world where I live, about personal relationship with Jesus, which is wonderful. We need that relationship with Jesus. But as Catholics, what is the locus of that relationship with Jesus Christ? It's in the *Eucharist*. Yet, sadly, Catholics today are fractured even over this basic belief that we have. In too many parishes they don't want to emphasize belief in the real presence: that the Lord of the universe, Jesus Christ who died on the cross and rose from the dead, is really present in what appears to our senses as consecrated bread and wine. They may not deny the real presence, but they don't mention it or go too deep into the mystery.

But ultimately you can't catechize in a parish that's not centered on the Eucharist. You can't build the unity necessary to form persons ready not only to withstand the world but to convert it.

This all points to why it's key for dioceses and for parishes to have faithful, liturgically reverent people ministering in them. If we have people on the payroll who are sort of compromise Catholics, who say, "Oh, the Church is full of baloney on contraception or marriage or abortion, but I'll put up with it because I like being Catholic"; if those people are the ones working in our parishes and diocesan offices (and there are many such scandalous stories), it creates contradictions that sap the life and unity of a Catholic community.

If the Church were only a human organization, this would be fatal. Thankfully, she is not. Here's where the rubber meets the road on Christ's promise—even all this disunity will not take down the Church. It may weaken and even destroy a lot of the institutional elements of the Church, but it's not going to take down the Church. Yet it will greatly weaken the Church and imperil souls.

If you're working for General Motors and you don't believe in the product—if you give customers reason to doubt it—the company suffers. The employees have to be on the same page for their product to succeed. Now, it may sound crass to talk about the Faith as a product, but there are principles from the business world that can be helpfully applied to catechesis and evangelization, and that's one of them.

In my pastoral work I have had great relationships with people involved in ministry. Then they have me over for dinner and I find out, "Oh, you also volunteer at Planned Parenthood?" or "Oh, you're going to a workshop on how to help people with gender transition? That's nice."

We can have the greatest love and kindness for those people and be mindful of how emotion gets involved and people feel rejected and all of those things. But we must reject the pastoral approach that puts such things ahead of truth and our duty to God's people. It doesn't matter if they're good people or if, for the most part, they convey Church teaching accurately.

Pastorally, I like Pope Francis's emphasis on accompaniment, absolutely. For people whose beliefs or lifestyle contradict Church teaching, we have to go out and accompany them along their way, remembering that they're precious children of God no matter what they're doing, no matter where they are. And sometimes you have to lovingly agree to disagree for a while and let God's grace work on them. God gives us time. In his mercy, he gives us opportunity after opportunity to live his truth. I think pastorally we need to do the same thing.

But to pay someone who is out on the street contradicting or undercutting Catholic teach-ing—that rises to different level from just deal-ing with the individual on his personal journey. It really ratchets up the stakes, not only because such a person is professionally bound to repre-sent Catholic teaching and practice faithfully, but because his salary is donated by people who can rightfully expect their dollars to be used in ways that fully support Catholic teaching.

In between those two are people who want to volunteer and often don't even fully realize how their beliefs or witnesses are a detriment to true ministry. They want to be faithful and they think they are being faithful, and they're shocked when you explain to them. I hate to say no to such people, and a lot of times they don't take it very well. That's a sad part of where we are also.

Catholic Education Must Embrace the Truth

To REALLY BE Catholic from the basement to the pinnacle of the roof, every aspect of everything that a Catholic school does needs to be imbued with the beauty of the Faith.

Sadly, too many Catholic schools today are more imbued with the secular culture. They're compromised, lukewarm; they have faculty living and teaching contrary to the Faith. They indulge the same educational fads and political enthusiasms that state schools do.

I believe it was Pope St. Paul VI who said something like, "People respond more to witnesses than to teachers." It may be an apocryphal quote, but the basic idea is sound: an audience is moved more by someone who is living the truth, not merely speaking it. This goes for young people especially. It's built into teenagers of whatever era—they have a barometer for phoniness and hypocrisy. Teenagers and young adults can see through that more quickly than anyone else.

And so in our Catholic high schools and universities that are Catholic in name only, compromised in what they're teaching, with teachers who don't witness to what they're saying in class, students sense the inauthenticity and are turned off by it. This makes them cynical and kills their faith. They decide that whatever they're going to believe, it won't be these silly Catholic myths that even their own teachers obviously don't buy.

And then, of course, a lot of what's being taught in Catholic universities, especially, just directly contradicts the Faith—whether it's skepticism about the supernatural or dismissing the Church's "antiquated" sexual morality. This is what the world is saying, what secular universities are saying, but it's even more damaging to students' faith when they hear it at a school whose "Catholic identity" gives it a presumption of authority.

But there are some good Catholic universities. How do we identify the ones that are truly Catholic? There are some tests we can apply.

Does the school's campus culture uphold a Catholic moral code as the norm for student life? A good Catholic college won't try to forcibly eliminate every sin on campus (which is impossible), but neither does it take a neutral, relativistic approach to moral life. It proclaims the ideal, upholds policies that encourage it, and supports students striving for it.

Does it teach people to *think*? University education should be more than a digestion of information—it should emphasize the tools of reason and reason's harmony with faith.

Does it educate the whole person for life? Learning how to reason not only helps you discern truth; it gives you a matrix of coping that can be adapted to every circumstance and period in your life. If you learn how to determine what really gives you long-term satisfaction and meaning, you have a template for sorting through whatever life throws at you. I think of Ignatius of Loyola's discernment of spirits. It applies not just to the spiritual but to every element of living as a human. A truly Catholic college education will leave a graduate prepared to live a fully human life.

The number of such colleges in the United States isn't great, but there are a number of good choices. I admit I'm partial to my alma mater, the University of Dallas. It's a small, truly Catholic university that exposes people to the beauty of what the Catholic faith offers and how it can build a wonderful human civilization, but it also is realistic about some of the brokenness that we still have to deal with.

At every level, Catholic education needs to embrace that supernatural truth more. We've got to be authentic and teach real, orthodox Catholic truth and not compromise out of a false sense of respect for other beliefs. Certainly, we should never show disrespect for anyone, but we must remember that the greatest respect is to bring people to the truth.

If they don't want the truth, okay. Christ said that if you go to a village and people don't want his message, shake the dust from your feet and move on. When he said, "You must eat my flesh and drink my blood to have life in you," a lot of people walked away, probably thinking he was crazy. But Jesus didn't say, "Please stay; I'll give you the option of pretending I didn't really mean that and it's just sort of symbolic." No, he didn't back off from the truth. And I don't think Catholic schools should, either.

One reason I think we've compromised too much is that we've become convinced that a compromised Catholic Church is more marketable. To say, "If you don't like it, you don't really *have* to go to confession to have your sins forgiven. Just go talk to the trees and they'll forgive you": this failure to give people credit for the ability to embrace hard teachings has been a disaster. And it's completely wrongheaded.

At one of the bishops' meetings recently, we had a presentation of a study that showed something that to me is pretty obvious. "If we want to bring young people back to the Catholic faith," it said, "back to the truth that we believe God has revealed to us, we've got to quit watering it down." There *is* a "market" for the orthodox Faith. Young people *do* want authentic, undiluted supernatural truth. They want to know the fullness of who Jesus Christ is and what he has revealed to us, and they want to see models of people living that faith with integrity.

If we live the truth and embrace it joyfully, if we don't just grudgingly say, "Ah, the Church ties our arms behind our backs all the time," that truth is going to set us free. It will make us flourish. And it will move us to truer and greater respect for every person, even those who reject everything that we believe. Our light will shine before them all the brighter.

Giving Meaning to the Mystery

YOUNG PEOPLE ARE attracted to the Church because they're looking for truth, looking for answers, looking to understand who we are and who God is and what this life's about. They grow up conditioned to believe that everything is explainable through science, but at some point they realize it's not. Scientists come up against mystery just as theologians do. Our faith doesn't fully explain it—because then it wouldn't be a mystery—but it gives the mystery meaning and, with it, our lives. And I think that's part of the attraction of a lot of young people to a more reverent, more theocentric liturgy.

Naturally, as human beings, we need order, we need structure, we need some kind of direction in life. And I think a lot of young people have grown up with basically none of that in their family and in society. And they're moving toward something that gives them some structure.

And that's good news. Yes, youth have struggles. Yes, there are challenges. But we know that the full gospel unlocks a joy in our lives that, though it doesn't instantly take away the world's problems or the confusions or the disappointments or our own sinfulness, gives us an anchor of hope and light that can pierce the darkness that so many young people are facing.

The latest darkness, of course, is the coronavirus pandemic and our society's response to it—churches shut down or suppressed and scary statistics on the news every day. But stretching back through the ages, there's always a threat of some kind. The good news of Jesus Christ is that no threat can overcome us.

The *True* Spirit of Ecumenism

I'VE OFTEN SAID weddings and funerals and presided in other settings where I knew there were numerous non-Catholics. We really have to honor the zealous faith of Evangelical Protestants. They are true disciples of Jesus Christ, often better Christians than we are—they're doing it with minimal rations! We have a banquet of sacraments and saints and history and liturgy and the Magisterium, and they just have (their own private interpretation of) the scriptures. And not even all the scriptures—the complete canon of the Bible came about through the authoritative discernment of the Catholic Church, and they reject parts of that canon.

One of the great fruits of Vatican II, one that didn't get tainted as much by the worldly "spirit," has been Scripture studies—a greater appreciation of how the Bible is our book. And even the liturgy has been enriched through greater exposure to Scripture than before the council.

So we've got everything in the banquet of supernatural truth in the Catholic Church, but although Evangelicals lack our provisions, many practice admirable faith and make great sacrifices to live it. Many of them have been staunch allies in defense of unborn life and in other battles between Christianity and the secular culture. I have visited with them in such efforts, and they're right there with us. Here in East Texas, on some of these issues Catholics are closer with their Evangelical Protestant brothers and sisters than they are with Catholics in some other parts of the country. On the life issues, on sexual morality, on the importance of traditional marriage, and on respect for this nation and its values, we are comfortable together as Catholics and Protestants. They are the salt of the earth.

Of course, what we believe about contraception is not even in their universe (with rare exceptions). "It's just one of those Catholic things" (even though it isn't). I pray, though, that as more of our Evangelical friends take note of the evil fruits of contraception, of the breakdown of families and of society, they may start to appreciate the coherence of Catholic sexual morality—how our beliefs about marriage, sex, and unborn life are all of a piece—and become closer allies still.

In fact, over the years I've had a number of people and ministers from Protestant churches talk to me about that. I try to convey to them that the truth is the truth. It's not Catholic truth versus Protestant truth. It's simply the truth. It is reality.

Ecumenism is great, and we want to be loving and friendly with everyone. But ultimately it has to be about more than static dialogue or mutual understanding—it has to be about returning all Christians, even all people outside of Christian communities, to full communion with the Church. It can't get stuck on "Well, you've got your truth and I've got my truth and we'll agree to tolerate our differences."

The Catholic Church is the Church Jesus established. The goal is for everyone to be part of his Church. I think when you're honest with yourself and others on this point, ecumenism as we have become used to practicing it kind of falls apart. I'm not going to become part of some other Christian group, and I'm not going to compromise what the Catholic Church teaches in order to get cozier with some other Christian group. The Catholic Church is an imperfect institution, but it is holy and it is true because the Holy Spirit animates and guides her. So the endgame of ecumenism, if it is authentic, Spirit-led ecumenism, has to be complete unity in the fullness of the faith we confess together.

Are there Anglicans or Methodists out there who believe that ultimately everyone in the world needs to be Anglican or Methodist? I doubt that's the approach they would take. So the kind of relativistic ecumenism that predominates, the kind that papers over differences and sets a low bar for similarities, seems more of a natural fit on the mainstream Protestant side. (Though of course there are Fundamentalists who think Catholics aren't even real Christians, so they probably aren't interested in that sort of ecumenism!)

But if you really believe what we believe—that the Eucharist really is Christ's body and blood, soul and divinity, and that Christ wants the whole world to be fed with it, not just the Catholic Club—then any goal short of that isn't good enough.

I've often said we tend to be too literally "cradle Catholics": we're asleep, dozed off in the beauty of what we just kind of inherited or stumbled into because we happened to be born into a family that had us baptized as infants and gave us the basics of the Faith. A lot of the strength of the Church today is in converts who have embraced the Catholic faith after a long journey; they value Catholicism more because they had to learn for themselves how it's of divine origin. They had to work through objections and the inertia of their former life and seize Catholic truth for their own, identify with it fully.

Many cradle Catholics, in contrast (and also some converts) have not had to "do the work" of studying and owning the Faith. Certainly, Catholicism is much more than just an intellectual enterprise, but the intellectual aspect is quite significant. Through study, we can come to really know who Jesus Christ is and what he has revealed to humanity. And of course, the Church began with adult converts! Many of her members who were contemporaries with Jesus never actually met him, but they came to know him by coming to know his teachings. So I think converts teach us a lot about how we should approach sharing the message of Jesus, the message of the Catholic Church, in today's world.

Yet it seems as if today in the Church there's too much of an anti-conversion attitude. "Let Protestants be saved by Protestantism and we'll be saved in our slightly different brand of Christianity." There's a loss of evangelical fervor, too, as was hinted at during the Amazon synod. "Let's not baptize anyone; instead, let's see what the Church can learn from paganism." Let's admire their idols and see what we have in common. We're not supposed to "proselytize," which is supposed to mean that we don't force the Faith on people, but it has functionally come to mean that we never try to convert anyone.

I think that's anti-Christian. It's not what Christ said, and it's not what I believe Christ calls us to.

If we don't really believe the Faith enough to share it, to shout it from the rooftops, to tell other people that Catholicism is true and what they believe is at least partly false, then honestly,

I quit. I don't want any part of an amorphous, homogenous, compromised glob that doesn't believe in much of anything. There's plenty of that in the world already. If the Church was just one among many such groups, I would have to go work at Walmart or something.

But from the depths of my soul I'm constrained from following any other path because I *do* believe that Christ is the answer and that the Church presents Christ in his fullness. And as long as I'm breathing, I will continue to hold up that full Christ, who, through the Church he founded, offers rest to the restless heart of every person in the world.

II

Leaven

✠ ✠ ✠

What a Catholic Can Do in This Crisis

What is the most basic answer to this crisis? Live your faith. Seek sanctity.

If you're a man, be a man of God. If you're into anything that is not chaste, manly son of God, get it out of your life. Make a good examination of conscience that really looks at what is going on in your life. Are you misusing the gift of your sexuality? Are you misusing the authority and power you have at work or in your family? Are you mis-using the wealth and the money that you have? Is it totally your god?" Just look at all three of those things in your own life. Sex, money, power. Abuses of those things are key vices that all of us struggle with in one way or another. Look at how these vices may have a hold on you, be honest with yourself, and strive to do better. When you fall, and we all do, go to confession, receive God's mercy, and get back to work with his grace.

If you're married, support your wife in her journey, too. Be an instrument of her salvation, as spouses should be for each other. And then look to the children. We have some young families that are on fire with the Faith and very dedicated and really trying to heal our culture, our nation, our Church, through their own sanctity. And I applaud them, and we need to support them.

I've talked to struggling parents, and I know that it is an uphill battle against a culture that thinks the Church is an antiquated, meaning-less institution. We're immersed in a culture that constantly steers us toward unbelief. But don't be afraid. First, grow in sanctity yourself and trust in the power of God's grace and the Holy Spirit. Be a light to your family and let the Holy Spirit leaven their souls. I've seen the transformations happen, and it's always according to God's will and God's time; just be as faithful as you can and trust in the Lord. You may not live to see the transforming grace that you're doing your best to promote in the lives of your children and your grandchildren, but don't lose heart.

To women I would likewise say: be a godly woman, chaste and committed to living a simple and holy life in the Lord. Reject the temptation of seeking power, which is an issue with some women today because of injustices that women have suffered in the past. I think that one of the things that's so overshadowed in our culture is the natural complementarity of a man and a woman. But that's what marriage is ultimately about. Marriage means men bring what women can't, women bring what men can't. Bringing that together creates family, creates the opportunity for children to thrive. It creates the domestic church. Men and women working together in a loving complementarity creates a microcosm of what the Church is supposed to be.

All the brokenness in our hearts and in the culture can seem like an insurmountable obstacle, but in faith it isn't. God can do all things, even with us. Never despair, never give up, never believe that it's too late or you can't do any good. We may not always see the good that we do. Make the Faith something that you're living in your own life, living in your home, and sharing with every life that you touch.

Then you will be like leaven in the world, catalyzing life and growth and renewal.

How to Be a Sign of Contradiction

FOR THE 500TH anniversary of the Protestant Reformation, which, for a lot of our neighbors here in East Texas, was a celebration of being freed from Rome and all of that, I placed a full-page ad in our Tyler newspaper to emphasize the need for Christian unity. I quoted John 17:21, where Christ prayed that his followers would be one. This is an issue not just among Christians but within the Church. There is a lot of disunity, and the efforts to be unified, as far as I'm concerned, have to be unified in the truth.

Let me share a story that, to me, shows the benefit of doing your best to teach the truth in love, as Jesus did.

I had a young family that moved into the Tyler area. The young man, a husband and father, is a physician. And he had been kind of going with the flow, going along with the norm of his profession in some ways that don't accord with Church teaching. Then someone had the courage and love to explain this to him, and ultimately he made the decision to change how he operated in his medical practice. He had to explain to his boss why he had to follow his faith and his conscience, and his family took a financial hit for making that choice.

To me, that's an illustration of how the truth does set us free. It doesn't necessarily make life easy or less complicated—often the opposite happens. But there will be abundant blessings in their lives because they're making the sacrifice to live the truth of the gospel.

If this young physician had come to me and said, "I heard the priest say this in a homily, and I'm upset. How dare you say that I can't do this or that and be a good Catholic!" That's not what happened, but if that's what had happened, the loving thing for me would still be to share the truth, to accompany him *in truth* as well as love, and hope that with grace and time he would come around.

Thankfully, there was no such confrontation except his own internal confrontation, in his conscience through his reflection and prayer. *Can I keep doing this if I want to really be a faithful Catholic?* And he came to his own conclusion, by the guidance of the Holy Spirit, to say, *No, I've got to change and I've got to make some sacrifices that are very real for my young family, but I've got to live the truth.*

You can apply that basic scenario to most of our lives. To live the truth fully takes courage and often comes with sacrifice—not always in money or material goods but sometimes in our families, or in our ambitions, or in our freedoms. Yet the rewards are joy and peace.

Of course, we all fail at times to do the good we ought, and we're all going to say and do things we ought not. But when our lives are systemically out of line with God's teachings, when we habitually, in our work or marriage (for instance), act in ways that are immoral, that's where a pastor's or a fellow Christian's loving reminder of the truth can set our consciences straight and steer us back to what is right.

Look back to Genesis and the people of Israel as you go through all of their story. It's a constant call of repentance and a demonstration of how God doesn't give up. His mercy is always there, giving his people the chance to repent, no matter how many times we resist it. That is the story of our relationship with God, who is always calling us to repentance, mercifully giving us another chance while we're dragging our feet. That's how it works.

Sometimes you will be accused of being a "divider" if you refuse just to go along with the majority when the majority is wrong, whatever the issue is. But this is the kind of division—to be a sign of contradiction to the world—that shows you're seeking to live the truth of the gospel. The culture says that more stuff will make us happy; be a sign that the stuff in your life is not where your happiness comes from. The culture says power is all important; be a sign that people are the most important elements of your daily life. The culture says sex is about the mutual pursuit of temporary pleasure; be a sign that sexual intimacy is about a man and a woman knowing each other deeply in a lifelong and fruitful bond.

So the idea that we should keep our mouths shut instead of "dividing," or the related idea that mercy comes before truth, is an insidious falsehood that is totally off the mark. You hear a lot of talk of mercy in the Church today, but it's described in a way that's only partially right. Unity presupposes truth, and mercy is always directed toward our eternal salvation.

@Bishopoftyler

I TWEET; A lot of people are aware of that! I've always said that St. Paul would have used Twitter if it had existed then. He used the communication tools of his day—letters and word of mouth. Today he would be tweeting, he would be doing podcasts, he would have a YouTube channel and a blog.

Social media has pitfalls, certainly. Sometimes I get off in the weeds or lose my temper. That's not helpful, and I try to avoid that, but it doesn't mean we should ignore all the light and truth we can share through these media. I believe we have to use the tools that the age gives us. The Church has always done this. Sometimes people point to the invention of the printing press as a point of unraveling for the Church, but that's shortsighted. On balance, the print medium has been of incalculable benefit in evangelization, catechesis, and apologetics. There's a mountain of helpful

Catholic material in print. Saints such as Maximilian Kolbe and communicators of the Faith such as Fulton Sheen used radio and television.

An advantage of using Twitter is that one can put gospel truth and ideas of faith into the information stream instantaneously. The clear *disadvantage* with Twitter and any modern social media is that it does not go deeply into any topic. That lack of depth can lead to misunderstanding and pushback. I try to use Twitter to bring light and leaven to the everyday conversation, but I always try to be on guard against inadvertently creating opportunities for opponents to shout down the message.

Is Benedict an Option?

THE WORLD PRESENTS a lot of spiritual dangers, but I don't believe it's the call of Christ to have a hunker-down mentality and to isolate ourselves. Married couples and families need to inject themselves with everything about the Faith that they can, in order to really become that intentional domestic church that they need to be, that they're called to be. Then they need to be leaven for the world—not put up fortress walls and take cover in their beautiful little domestic church; that is the opposite of what Jesus said.

The challenge we have is even greater than that, and the rewards richer. Families: absolutely be strong; have a center of faith, a center of love and support from which to meet the challenge of living the good news out in the world. The "pause" that much of the world has been on during the pandemic may afford, for some, a time of discernment and renewal, to practice being more intentional about living the Catholic truth. But we'll have to go out again, and again take the good news *to* the world.

None of us chose this task, but it has been thrust upon us. God chose the *laity* especially for this mission—to go out into the culture and leaven it, make it rise.

Again I say to families: be that center of faith and loving support from which your family members draw strength for the mission. That source to which they can go, not to hide, but to be rejuvenated, strengthened again, edified, and corrected against the errors and temptations of the world; from which they can then go back out to the world and bring Christ to it.

Even among faithful Catholics I think that there can be a tendency to despise this world too much. It happened in the early Church with some of the heretical movements that said, "Oh, well, this life really doesn't matter. We might as well just commit collective suicide and move on to the kingdom." But that's not God's plan.

The opposite is the truth: the more this life can be sanctified, the more we can be leaven in the world, and the closer we move toward the everlasting kingdom that is our destiny. As soon as we're baptized, that becomes our mission, both individually and together as the Church, and we have to embrace it.

I use the word *joy* a lot because I think we tend to forget so easily that joy is meant to be experienced even in this world. It's easy to forget because life is such a challenge. There is evil in the world. We're sinners who mess up and get lost. Most of us don't hop out of bed every day singing "Oh, What a Beautiful Morning!" We acknowledge that joy is always going to be tarnished with our sin and the sin of others in a world of disharmony. But our weakness and the brokenness of the world don't mean we stop looking for and believing that the truth of Christ is about joy in this life.

If you go back to the *Baltimore Catechism*, it tells us who we are and what we're supposed to do: know, love, and serve God in this life and be happy with him in the next. People may ask,

"Does that mean there's no happiness here?"

No.

The *fulfillment* of happiness, the perfection of happiness, will be only in the next world. But this world prefigures the next, and God wants us to be joyful missionaries, joyful workers in building his kingdom here, today, in a world that Christ loves and we should, too.

Signposts for the Human Journey

SOME PREACHERS PRESENT a feel-good gospel that doesn't talk about sin. But I think one of the most uplifting things we can contemplate is the very stark and clear acknowledgment that we're sinners and need Christ's light. When we abandon ourselves to his mercy, we know we're not alone. It's not only central to the gospel to acknowledge the truth that we're not perfect and we need God's grace— it's enormously comforting and encouraging.

And so, if many Catholics are depressed and in a crisis of faith in these days, a big reason may be that we have lost this healthy, positive sense of sin.

Of course, that loss of a sense of sin may stem from an approach to morality that views sin as breaking something in God's rule book; that God's a tough dad with a long list of do's and don'ts, just waiting for us to screw up so he can punish us.

But that's a caricature of sin and of God the Father. I try to teach what sin is by asking, *What's going to break us? What is harmful to our nature? What is poisonous to the joyful life that God wants us to have?* That's sin. It can be the venial sin that's just a little poison, but it's still poison, that worms its way into our souls bit by bit. Or it can be the mortal sin that literally kills our souls, kills our joy, and destroys us. And we see it constantly unfolding in people's lives: virtue, bringing joy and strength, and sin, bringing misery and weakness.

Still, people say, "Oh, you Catholics have so many rules."

But it's not the Church that invented our moral laws. Those laws stem from the nature God created us with, and God gives us positive commandments based on those laws as signposts for living the human journey in a healthy way. They're the operation manual for mankind. When we violate a commandment, even in a way that is not serious, it diminishes our lives. And *that* is how we have to understand and talk about sin. God is not a tough dad waiting for us to slip up––he's an all-loving Father who wants us to live in a way that will makes us happy and fully human.

Healthy Marriages Will Heal the World

IF YOU GO back to the Arian heresy, you'll see that a majority of the bishops were Arian. In the 1960s, many, if not a majority of, bishops rejected *Humanae Vitae*. It was a marker for the sexual revolution. So it's not a surprise that today you see a lot of polls about how Catholics have rejected that teaching.

I think the Church's emphasis on the moral teachings of sexuality is so important or highlighted so much because it is so vital.

The sexual revolution has done very serious damage to humanity. I think people are going to say, as we look back on this sexual revolution from a more distant future, that it really messed up humanity.

To repair the damage, we must start with helping people be formed to really live what marriage is, because marriage is the only place where sexual life is lived in a healthy way. One of the best things that I got out of Pope Francis's document *Amoris Laetitia* was a beautiful emphasis on what I call a *remote* formation for marriage. People need a good lived experience, beginning as young children and continuing into early adulthood, of the characteristics of conjugal love and the habits of a loving marriage. That's the only way they'll know, as they approach marriage themselves, what it truly is—naturally, a fruitful, loving, complementary, lifelong partnership of a man and a woman, and sacramentally, a sign of Christ's love for his Church. It's also a cooperation with God in procreating the human family and ordering human society.

Those of us in the clergy who aren't married also need to understand the treasure that marriage is and to pray for married couples. You won't have a strong domestic church, you won't have that remote formation for marriage, if husbands and wives are living fractured relationships. So much of our brokenness in the world today stems from those fractures—from divorces and from marriages that don't model the truth of what they are.

And, of course, today we have the idea that two men or two women and even other "configurations" can be marriages. Yet these quasiconjugal relationships are broken by their very nature; they're not healthy, they're not going to flourish on the human level, and they can't be signs of what marriage means on the sacramental level. They're not healthy human relationships even before you bring immoral sexual aspects into the picture.

So we've got to really emphasize what it means to be a man and a woman and what it means for a man and a woman to become one flesh. The whole Catholic community—bishops and pastors, teachers and leaders, all the laity—needs to understand and embrace the meaning of marriage and then to defend and spread that good news within the culture.

Even if you don't believe that marriage is a sacrament, its basic components are the fabric of human civilization, not just of the domestic Church. When you don't have a man and a woman, one man and one woman committed for life in marriage, loving each other and open to bearing and raising children, things go haywire. All you have to do is look out your window and see how things are haywire with broken marriages, with single parents, with kids who are lost and not being directed. So both the remote and the continuing formation for marriage are essential.

And you know what? It's good news. It's challenging, but people are overjoyed to hear it. Many engaged couples—especially when they're not both Catholic—can be pretty much oblivious to the idea of why contraception is wrong. Many won't be converted overnight on this point. But the overall message of Christian marriage is compelling—especially when set against the backdrop of our current society's familial breakdown and sexual misery. More people are realizing that our society has been sold a bill of goods: that sexual license is really slavery, that the liberation promised by the Pill turned out to be heartache and health problems.

So we've got to teach the world, and we start by teaching our own couples who are preparing to marry in the Church. And frankly, that's why I can get really furious when I see pastors or teachers in the Church promoting contraception and other aspects of immoral sexual behavior or glossing over them. When *Humanae Vitae* was promulgated, there were clergy and theologians openly rejecting it: in the *New York Times*, in classrooms, from the pulpit. Sadly, today we continue to reap the fruits of their dissent.

And so who can blame Catholics today for not understanding the fullness of Catholic teaching on marriage? The Church let them down.

Here I can speak very honestly about my own personal journey. I was rector of the cathedral here in Tyler for sixteen years, and I always believed and tried to teach what the Church taught: that contraception was not moral and was to be avoided. But I didn't teach it clearly or frequently enough or with any vigor. If somebody nailed me to the wall and said, "Okay, Father Joe, is contraception moral or not?" I would have given the Church's teaching. But I didn't preach on it or try to get that message out to the people. It was too controversial. And in my training for the priesthood, I was taught to keep people happy and not to ruffle feathers. And if that's your goal, then you're going to avoid saying the tough things. I did the same in confession with individuals.

Now, as bishop in that same cathedral, I'm trying hard to meet that pastoral challenge to focus on this teaching and how it is good news, a truth that people need to have. I'm much more focused on teaching the hard stuff because any loving father knows that kids need to be challenged so they can grow and be happy and flourish in this life. Of course, there are pastors and even bishops who would totally disagree with everything I just wrote—who think that sooner or later the Church will wake up and discard her outdated teachings on sex and marriage. As far as I'm concerned, hogwash. The truth is the truth.

Th truth about our sexuality is also so intimate and central to who we are. It's not the *totality* of who we are, but it is intimately woven into how we live out our lives. And I know it's painful to people who are facing same-sex attraction or other kinds of issues in their marriages, so I've tried to be very clear that bigotry toward anyone because of any struggle he has is always wrong. That is not of Christ. But we don't overcome bigotry or harsh judgmentalism by saying that immoral acts are perfectly fine; to me, that's not mercy but a deeper bigotry. It's denying the truth to people who desperately need it.

Thankfully, the *Catechism of the Catholic Church* is very clear on all of these issues, even if some leaders and teachers of the Church are not so clear—even saying out loud that what the *Catechism* says needs to change. For example, that word it uses in regard to sexuality that is not according to the marriage plan of one man and one woman: *disordered*. "It's too harsh," some say. Even "harmful."

But rather than erasing this word and denying people important, healing truths, we should emphasize how *all* sexual sin is in a sense disordered, since it turns away from the natural purpose of sex within a marriage. Masturbation is disordered, pornography is disordered, hooking up is disordered. Polyamory is disordered. Ninety-nine percent of the sex presented in popular entertainment is disordered.

But as believers, we need to work toward ordering our lives according to the good news of Jesus Christ. That's what the beauty of Church teaching on sex, in its bold fullness, shows us: how to order our most intimate selves in the way that pleases God and leads us to happiness and fulfillment.

Marriage Is for Life

MARRIAGE—THE INSTITUTION in which women learn to be fully women and men learn to be fully men—is one key way that the laity can help pull us out of this formless wasteland that the world has become. Only through the witness of strong, loving, selfless marriages will we begin to repair the brokenness at the root of so many of our society's problems. Some may say this is impossible, as marriage has been redefined and rates of marriage plummet, but nothing is impossible with

God. Indeed, one of the greatest signs of hope that I see in my diocese is the increasing number of strong new marriages.

We need to water these seeds of hope, supporting married couples and families and adding to their numbers. This is the front line of the battle that we're facing to bring the world back to God's plan for the salvation of humanity. That's why Satan hates marriage so much and puts so much effort into weakening and destroying families. And make no mistake: the anti-marriage, anti-family forces in this world are diabolical. The devil and his demons hate mankind, and they know that if you pervert marriage, you destroy the seedbed of human civilization, which is built on one marriage and one family at a time.

How can we thwart the devil's efforts? All we can do is turn to Christ: to beg his graces upon couples and families and to invite him to work through us to help them build Catholic homes and a Catholic civilization that will repair our broken culture.

But that is a huge task and, and frankly a lot of the Church isn't on that task.

We need to have ideals as Catholics and as followers of Jesus Christ. What he lays out for us is an idealistic way of life that isn't easy. You don't just sort of fall over and it happens. You've got to put human effort into it. And it's the same thing for marriage and formation for marriage. Pope Francis has emphasized that marriage formation actually begins long before a couple is engaged. It begins in one's own family, which is a school of love. And it continues in the pastoral witness of the Church. Everything we do and teach as a Church should be forming Catholics to wield the tools of love and self-sacrifice, by which all strong marriages are built.

But we know that all marriages aren't strong, and many break apart. Why? At the beginning, the couples are obviously saying they love each other and want to spend their lives together. They sincerely plan to raise a family together. They profess vows in my presence and in the presence of the Church, saying this is for life. And then it ends in divorce. They have the best intentions, but then they run into something called life that gets hard. Life doesn't unfold the way they thought it would. It happens over and over again, and it's heartbreaking.

I think in the culture, when something's not working, the attitude is to dispose of it and get something else. We acquire and discard *things* so easily in the modern world, so why not people? It's an insidious mindset, one that sadly is only marginally less common in the Catholic community than in the general population. How do we change this? How do we intervene to give couples the best possible chance of avoiding the disposable-marriage mentality?

I think we start, when people come in for marriage preparation, by taking them at their word. You say you are deeply in love with each other? I believe you. Now, *here's what that love really means.* It means more than you realize, perhaps more than you can imagine. It means you are committed to be faithful to each other for life. It means a commitment to this permanence through bad times—bad times you can't even conceive of now—as well as good. It means a willingness to open up your love and let it be fruitful, let it grow beyond the two of you into a family that will share and magnify your love. It means learning to love each other more and more as life goes on.

Every year around World Marriage Day, we have in the diocese a Mass for couples celebrating five, ten, or fifty years of marriage. We had a couple who had celebrated *seventy-five years* of marriage this year. We asked that couple,

"How have you done this? How did you stay married for so long?" And I love the answer. It's so down-to-earth. They simply said, and in that good, plain, East Texas way, "Neither of us died. We're both still alive. We said 'till death do us part.' And we're still here."

All the fancy couples' psychology in the world isn't as helpful as beginning marriage by committing to that simple, stubborn fact: *this is for life.*

Yes, life gets rough. Life gets disappointing. Life gets tragic. And so the mindset that we have to help couples who are approaching marriage to have is to say, yeah, life's going to get hard. But not only are you called to sustain your marriage through the hard times—the grace of the sacrament of marriage will sustain *you* through the hard times. It is there to help you to sustain *each other* through the hard times. Marriage isn't just something that you fight and work *for*; it's something that *gives you* the strength to fight and work—the strength to love.

The Preeminent Social Issue
of Our Time

AT A NOVEMBER meeting of the U.S. bishops, we discussed whether the word *preeminent* should still be used as we speak about abortion. I stood up and said that it must be. As Catholics, we must believe that the sanctity of life is the preeminent issue of our time. Abortion is murder of the most vulnerable, the weakest, the tiniest of those on the spectrum of human life—how can it not be preeminent?

In Texas, as in many other parts of the country, there's a lot of concern about immigration. The border has been a mess for half of my life. And absolutely, that's a human rights issue, that's a sanctity of life issue. But we can't lose the focus and put all of our emphasis there and forget that throughout the country, throughout the world, life is being snuffed out in mothers' wombs, and morally as well as a matter of policy, that is a graver and clearer issue. Abortion is not just the preeminent political issue of the moment in our country; it is the preeminent issue of our time in the whole world.

Some of my fellow bishops did debate this on the floor of the USCCB. Some said that we shouldn't use this language, that it goes against what Pope Francis has said. Thankfully, one of the *ad limina* groups of American bishops later reported that Pope Francis confirmed abortion's preeminence as a human rights issue. Still, some of the bishops of the United States do seem to want to de-emphasize abortion and place it among other social issues in importance.

But I think it's important to keep our focus on abortion. That's why I tweet about it—which I try to do with as much light and love as possible. We need to push back against a culture that says it's a "right" to destroy unborn life. And even though we all know what social media is like, it still really amazes me—the ugly, filthy language that gets thrown at you for saying it's wrong to kill a child in the womb. Calling me a bigot, saying I just want more children so I can sexually abuse them . . . It's just a sad commentary on where our society is.

Abortion is wrong, but a lot of things are wrong that aren't that serious. Abortion is more than wrong—it's murder of the most heinous kind. I admit that I get emotional about it sometimes. We've got to wake up to the evil of abortion.

I write this in the middle of 40 Days for Life. Not long ago, a reporter approached me as we were praying in front of a clinic and asked, "What are you here for?"

"We're just praying for the women and the children," I answered, "for the families that are involved in this tragedy of abortion."

Then something dawned on me as I spoke to her, and I said, "Our approach is that you're always dealing with two people. You've got the woman and the child in her womb. That's two persons, two human beings." Then I realized we need to really embrace it even more fully, and I said, "Let me correct myself. We're dealing with *three* people. We're dealing with the mother, we're dealing with the child in her womb, and we're dealing with the man who is the father of that child."

That was a moment of clarity for me. For years, the accusation against pro-lifers was that we care about this unborn child but not about the woman. Absolutely, we need to care about both, and in that area I think the Church has made progress and society has made progress.

And if we can help a woman see that the life in her womb is sacred, is a separate person who deserves the right to be born, then we've got to step up and support her, too.

But a lot of the brokenness of abortion is on the *man,* too—even if he just showed up long enough to impregnate this woman and then was gone, or if there's a broken relationship, or whatever. So, I think it's important for us as a Church and as a society to say, "Okay, where's the man? How do we support him?" As with the Gospel account of the woman caught in adultery, the man may not be on the scene, but he's still part of the story.

I could talk for a long time on the crisis of manhood in our culture. It has huge implications for marriage; it has huge implications for family; it has huge implications just for human society. Too many men are not living as godly men. They're not living up to the manly call to be responsible for their actions; they're not part of the lives of their children; they're caught up in pornography or substance addiction or addiction to their careers.

I'm going to keep speaking up as long as I'm able to on abortion and on womanhood and manhood. The future of the Church and the world are closely connected with these things.

Satan and Demons

EVEN SIMPLY FROM logic, if you believe in good, there has to be evil. If you see the light, it's because it shines in the darkness. Even pagans understood this. At Easter, what are we singing hallelujah about, really? What does it come down to? It's that Jesus Christ, God's divine Son, conquered evil by his death and resurrection. He crushes the head of the serpent.

If, even as a bishop, I talked too deeply about Satan and demons, I'd probably be carted off in a straitjacket. But their existence is part of the supernatural truth we embrace. They're real. They lost; they've been conquered by Jesus; but they're real, and they want to hurt us by leading us to sin. Every sin opens the door a little wider to evil and error.

As a priest, I've been contacted numerous times by people needing help: a call or knock on the door at 3 a.m. from people thinking there are demons inside them or in their houses. Usually they don't need an exorcist, just as most people who are a little sick don't need brain surgery. In the spiritual realm we have to discern symptoms just as a doctor does.

Are there natural causes? Often it turns out there's turmoil in the family. There's sinful behavior—cohabitation or drugs or violence, or playing around with a Ouija board, all of which can invite demonic activity. So you start asking questions and try to pull them back from the sinful behavior, from the ways they're tiptoeing into some dark areas of reality. You pray with them, bless them and their home with holy water. As Christ says, all power in heaven and on Earth has been given to him by the Father, and that includes authority over their sinful habits and, yes, the demons who tempt and oppress them.

Yes, Satan and his angels are real, and they are having a field day with so many things going on today. The Catholic Church has been brought to her knees, not in prayer but in humiliation—over the abuse crisis and recently over the widespread closing of churches during the pandemic. Sin has consequences. The more the world moves into the darkness of relativism, where everyone's a God and everyone can decide what's true, the more Satan's hatred for us meets its purpose.

We need to be sober and alert to the reality of evil. But always in the context that ultimately,

Christ has conquered evil in its every manifestation. He has won the day. That's what we celebrate in his resurrection, that he has conquered sin and death. He has brought the light of the Father and the grace of the Holy Spirit into the world to stay. That is reality. That is where we are. But our sinfulness can distort that and mess things up, which it does all the time.

The Right Approach to Social Justice

SINCE THE WORLD is undeniably messed up, it begs to be healed. The Church offers medicine for healing, even in the temporal sphere; but this is not the Church's first job. Some Catholic leaders, even some other bishops, disagree with me to one extent or another on the Church's core mission. A sizable part of the Church, especially in my lifetime, see the Church as an institution of social workers going out and trying to bring justice to the streets and trying to change and reform everything in this world.

And that certainly has its place. There is injustice in the world, there are social ills, and we're called to bring the truths of the gospel to bear on these issues, too.

But I don't want to belong to a club or an activist organization; I want to follow Jesus Christ. So issues related to our faith come first. This is my own opinion, and it comes from my prayer, but I think the Church has gotten off-track, flipped the order upside down. The universal call to holiness not only precedes but is the only thing that can bring to success to our efforts to end human trafficking and racism, cure societal ills such as drug abuse, and make our air and water cleaner.

Take the whole list of problems on Earth—it's endless. *Jesus Christ is the answer to everything on that list.* Before we get to the need for effective political policy, to charitable ministry, to prudent administration of the world's goods—all of which are necessary—Jesus must come first.

And I think that churches must be bold in saying that Jesus Christ is the answer. This may sound idealistic. People might reply, "We'll never get anywhere like that." But I believe we'll never get anywhere saying that the Church's main job is to reform laws or influence politicians, or even to feed the hungry. If we're reformers, we're reformers of souls and lifestyles. If we're influencers, our job is to influence the world to follow Christ. If we want to feed the world, first we feed it with the body of Christ.

Even when it comes to abortion, the greatest injustice in the world, there has been a lot of ink spilled, a lot of energy exerted, a lot of money spent; it's a huge, huge project of the Church. I don't disagree with this effort. But my first job as a pastor is to convert hearts to Christ. It belongs first to the laity to drive pro-life activism, craft legislation, and otherwise engage the temporal struggle to bring justice to the unborn.

That is what I believe. So much of the energy of the Church is focused on the human endeavor. But I think the Faith teaches that Christ is the answer to everything. He's the Lord of creation. He has all power in heaven and on Earth. I know that a lot of Catholics, a lot of bishops, would say this isn't realistic, that we have to get down in the trenches. And certainly, we can't ignore that people are hungry, that babies are being murdered in the womb, that the borders are a mess, all of those things, but I firmly believe that a pastor's first job is to focus on converting the hearts of the flock and sending them out to do the things that the gospel talks about.

So too often we get things kind of reversed. And ironically that makes our temporal efforts less effective. For when people have a relationship with Jesus Christ, when their hearts are converted, when they live by gospel values, when they are guided by Catholic moral teaching—*then* they're going to do justice and pass good laws. If they're close to Christ, *then* they will feed the hungry, protect the environment, treat other people fairly regardless of race, and pursue every other temporal good.

With social upheaval all around us, it can be tempting for bishops and priests to focus more on doing the social work. But it's our job to convert hearts and let the laity go do the social work in the world, as Vatican II says is their "special obligation" (*Apostolicam Actuositatem* 7). But with all these huge structures and departments and people earning big salaries, all focused on worldly reform, we risk leaving Christ out of the picture.

I'm not the most popular guy in the USCCB. But it's not my job to be popular with a group of bishops; rather, it's to teach and sanctify the flock under my care.

The Antidote to Racism

As we watch increasing violence in our streets and increasingly ideological conflict among our countrymen, it seems that so much stems from the fallen human tendency not to reflect, not to think, but to react emotionally. I think about Mary, who pondered things in her heart. As someone who has engaged on social media, I can say that there doesn't seem to be a lot of pondering going on there. It's a lot of reacting; it's a lot of emotions. We've lost the art of patient pondering and replaced it with instantaneous reaction.

What if instead we took a breath and said a prayer and then asked ourselves, what's the right thing here? Certainly, there's always injustice in the world, and it needs to be addressed. There are all kinds of issues that certainly need to be brought into the light and be made better. We should always be about living holier lives, and that means praying and then acting. It's not just about believing; it's what you do with that belief. It's not just about praying; but it's about how you act after you've taken some time to ponder and reflect and ask God to send his Holy Spirit to guide you.

Certainly, racism is one of the evils that we deal with. But rather than pointing the finger at other people or at "systems," perhaps we could ask ourselves, *okay, where's my sin?* Where do *I* need to make reparation? How can I repair rash judgments I've made and biases I've acted on in the past and avoid them in the future?

I also think that there are a lot of issues that get lumped in with racism when they're really rooted elsewhere. Which is why I am skeptical about activist groups supposedly working for racial or social justice that also advocate the destruction of the nuclear family. Do they really not see that the destruction of family life, especially black family life, is a big part of the problem, not the solution? Take away moms and dads committed to each other and to raising children in a community of love, break up that natural unit and leave children to be raised (usually fatherless) in its tattered remains, and you have a recipe for the poverty and crime that plague minority communities.

It's hard to believe they don't see it. So they want the nuclear family replaced with . . . what? What other kind of family is there? Get rid of it, and the void can be filled only by the state. It's kind of frightening.

Other activists for racial justice tie their cause to the redefinition of marriage and "gender," as if the basic human right to just treatment and equality before the law, which people of all races possess, were of a piece with a supposed right to tear down and reconstruct natural reality about sex, which no one has the right—or ability—to do.

The political side of all this conflict is complicated and has to be navigated shrewdly. But fortunately, the personal side, which comes first, is much simpler. We should pray together; we should have conversations; we should get to know each other better. We must examine ourselves for any habits of rash judgment of others based on race. God willed a diverse humanity. People of all races bring a richness of gifts and differences and qualities that should, in God's plan, enhance the human community. Let us work against reactionary impulse and work in favor of conversation, of praying together, of healing human interaction. Let us also work together for common goals. Racism melts away as we recognize and strive to meet the shared needs and ends of our common humanity.

This is one reason why the Church is well positioned to be an antidote to racism. We are a universal church, not a white or black or Latino church. Catholicity transcends race, language, and nationality. We all belong to it regardless of where we come from, and thus we all belong to one another as in a family. That's part of Catholicism's beauty, the beauty of God's plan for a harmonious working together toward conversion and salvation. Its diversity, united in a single purpose, enriches the whole.

The lack of faith in our post-God society works against this unity and makes racism worse by denying that we're one human family created equal in the image of God. That fundamental aspect of Christian anthropology is so simple but so essential! Take away God's creation of humanity and our shared relation to him and to one another, and you're left with competing social and political tribes with no real, lasting foundation for cooperation. We're not really one human family but just a collection of coalitions trying to achieve dominance over one another. And so atheism leads to division and strife of the kind that's intensifying at this moment; only shared belief in God's fatherhood can heal division and foster peaceful accord.

It sucks the meaning out of life—and it sucks the hope out of any attempt to overcome racism and promote justice.

Read the four Gospels and just look at what Jesus does. He's constantly going out to the disenfranchised. He's constantly reaching out to the poor—the materially poor, the spiritually poor, and those rejected by society. Even those who don't believe in Jesus's divinity can admit that he provides a laudable example of how humans should treat each other. And it's a revolutionary picture—I mean, *love your enemies*? Talk about a revolution. Seven billion people loving their

enemies would bring justice to the world overnight, and that's what Jesus Christ is about, if we
just look to him.

Relativism and the Real Presence

WE'RE LIVING IN a world where everyone cries,
"You can't tell me what to believe!" Well,
that's true, we really can't, but I think we need
to explore what the *truth* is. As Catholics, we
have a beautiful heritage of revealed truth. The
Catholic Church is all about revelation of truth.
We didn't figure this out on our own. It wasn't
a few popes and bishops deciding to make up
a religion. We are inheritors and guardians of
revealed truth from God.

In so many areas of our culture, though,
there's a tendency to say, "That's your truth,
and I'll have my truth, and we'll all just get
along." But history shows, and current events

are showing right now, that it doesn't work that way. If we're not guided by the same truth, then the fabric of civilization rips.

Is marriage something that's only between one man and one woman? Is it an indissoluble union of persons? Or it is a fluid thing that can include any combination of sexes and numbers and that lasts only as long as you want it to? It can't be both, and any culture that tries to have both will quickly realize it has to pick one and suppress the other.

This relativism infects the Church, too. We've all read and heard these surveys that huge percentages of Catholics don't even believe in the real presence. Frankly then, they're more Protestant than Catholic.

Either Christ meant it when he said in the Gospels (and as he's quoted in the writings of Paul), "Take this bread, it is my body. Take this wine, it is my blood," or he didn't. Either that's

real or it's not. It can't be both. Yet we live in a
world where we act as if it can be both, according to what someone wants it to be. But it can't
be one thing for you and another for me. And
it can't be both real presence and mere symbol
at the same time. We have to choose, and that
choice has consequences.

Waste Some Time in the
Lord's Presence

I TRY NOT to be one of those people who says,
"Everything has to be about this or that act of
piety." But if I were to promote a "pet project,"
it would be eucharistic devotion—because
everything has to be about Jesus Christ, and the
Eucharist is what it's all about. I get emotional
about it because by it I've come to know him in
ways that I didn't know him before. It probably
sounds corny, as if I think I'm really mystical,

but honestly, I don't feel mystical at all, just immeasurably blessed to know the Lord Jesus Christ in his real presence.

His presence is real. And I can tell you that as I leave his presence, there's a little part of me I leave behind, as if I'm missing a friend. I've never been married, but I imagine it's how a couple who are deeply in love and have a really blessed marriage feel when they're separated. That's the feeling I get when I leave the presence of Christ in the Blessed Sacrament. I've come to know him much more deeply than ever before.

I still get lazy about putting in time before the Blessed Sacrament. I'm still far from the sanctity that we're all called to, but adoration puts me more on the road to it than I've ever been before.

I know it scares people off. *I don't know what to do; I don't know what to say.* People are busy, and adoration can feel like a waste of time. But

I encourage people just to get over it. Get over your frustration or embarrassment when you're before the Lord and you don't think you're doing anything especially holy or fruitful. Get over your preconceptions about praying efficiently and just go ahead and "waste" some time in the presence of Christ. Do it enough, and you'll come to find that it's not fruitless and it's not wasted time. Even if you don't say a single prayer. Even if you doze off.

Yes, it's so antithetical to our modern culture just to sit there in silence and do nothing for more than an hour—or more than one minute! It drives us crazy. So it's not easy at first. It takes practice to let some of those expectations fall by the wayside and just *be* there in the Presence. Our brains "run hot," and we need to let them cool down.

Try this: start by just taking deep breaths and counting them. Try to get to twenty before you let your mind kick in. If we can get to twenty breaths of cooling silence, I think we will find prayer, just being quiet with God, much easier.

I think the best answer I can give for those who are wanting to seek that feeling of grace in their lives is to commit to real, regular prayer. That scares a lot of people. How am I supposed to do that? What form does it take in my life— liturgical prayer, *lectio divina,* adoration, meditation? I'm not holy enough . . .

But give it some time. Give it some time. Again, back to the fundamentals. Just as we need hours of exercise to see improvement in our fitness—and at the start it's jerky and awkward, and we feel silly—we need hours and hours of practice at prayer. If you put the time in and keep practicing, you will gradually get a rhythm; you will get a feel for it. It will become second nature, and you will become aware of the results in your life.

It'll be frustrating. You'll be tempted to say, "I'm not getting anywhere." But pray the rosary, read Scripture, simply sit in the eucharistic presence of the Lord, and I'll guarantee you'll start to feel some changes in your life. Everything really does flow from prayer: greater peace, greater clarity, greater knowledge, greater love, greater joy.

The End of the World

ALL THE AWFUL things going on in our country and in the world have a lot of people wound up, thinking about the end times and wondering if we're entering some kind of prophesied age. In response, I say simply that we have to look again to Christ. He dealt with the apocalyptic question in his time, and he said that's for the Father to know and for us not to worry about—except to live in a way that keeps us ready for his return.

So is this the beginning of the end of the world, for real? Let's get over that question and focus on the important one: when is *your* world going to end? Is today the day when *you* go before Christ in judgment? Are you paying attention to the signs in your own life? This way of thinking really brings home what following Jesus Christ is about.

My world could end in an hour. I'm not expecting it to, but it could. Yours could end before noon tomorrow. Are you ready? That's where the rubber meets the road. Don't lose sleep mentally piecing together signs of the apocalypse. Live in this world as Christ has taught us, reaching out with love and care to all of God's people and working to build Christ's kingdom with the assumption that there will be thousands of years before he comes again. But we should be constantly mindful of the imminent end of our world and our readiness for it.

So I think we have it backward. We get all bothered wondering if this or that event means the world's end is coming, but we pay little attention to the end of our personal world, which is guaranteed to happen sometime and could happen any time. *Memento mori,* the monks used to say—remember your death. It's a sobering thought, which is probably part the reason why it's not much emphasized in the Church today.

But it's the traditional perspective of the Church, so that means it's not a downer, not a dark message. It means just being alert and being aware that this world is a *temporary* home. We're on a journey to somewhere else, somewhere permanent, our true common home.

As John Paul II said right after his election and many times after that, *Be not afraid.* What I think he was getting at was that this is Christ's world. All power in heaven and on Earth has been given to him. When we remember that, it gives us power. Then we can stop worrying about the world and just choose to start listening to God more closely. We can commit ourselves to daily conversion.

How can I be a godlier person? How can I live the gospel virtues more clearly? Once we adopt that mindset, then there's really nothing to be afraid of, because this world is passing away. For some, it will be a beautiful journey, but whatever this world offers us, it's passing away all the same.

There's some joy in that, isn't there, the thought that we're not going to be here forever? This life gets pretty tedious at times—something we're all aware of lately with this crazy virus. Just as people can handle the lockdowns and social distancing for only so long and still keep their sanity, there's a limit to how much of life in this fallen world we can endure. *Memento mori* is not a message of darkness, or even principally a warning. It's a message of *hope* that after this vale of tears there lies something better and everlasting for those who believe in Jesus Christ.

Final Thoughts from a Texas Shepherd

WE TALK ABOUT believing: about faith that God exists, that he sent his Son, that he reveals his truths to us. All of that. But how much do we believe that these things are really real—as real as the computer screen I'm staring at? How much do we act as if the objects of our faith are really real?

I would never say, "Well, I believe that this is a computer screen, but it may actually be a loaf of bread. So if you want to believe that, okay." You would call me crazy if I did, because the reality is that this is a computer screen. It has the look and function, the design and molecules and atomic makeup of a computer screen.

That's reality. Can we approach faith in Jesus Christ, in what he has taught us, with that same confidence?

Can we find the courage to stand up and say, for instance, that marriage is between one man and one woman for life, open to children? That isn't an opinion. That isn't a belief. That is what God's plan for human beings is. That is marriage. That is reality.

When we decide we have a different opinion from reality, we get messed up, and that's where we are.

This certainly didn't begin with the Protestant Reformation, but it was a significant moment when a large number of Christians decided that they didn't believe in the reality of the Church any longer—that they would instead give primacy to their own private judgment about their personal reading of Scripture. Once you have replaced the objective order of reality with personal opinion, even collective opinion, the trouble starts.

And that's where we are. I know it can be so difficult in this culture to have a mindset that is Catholic and focused on truth and reality. We feel like aliens in this world. This disconnect hinders our ability to witness to what we believe and to bring people along to see it themselves—even though it's so basic and so clear to us! And we can get *really* frustrated when people in the Church say, "Oh, well, this or that may change." *We can't change reality.* If it is reality, we can't change it, and bad things happen when we act as if we can.

Sometimes, to blow off steam, I'll say something facetious like, "You know, I think we need to get a committee together and reconsider gravity. It's an outdated concept that doesn't fit our progressive age. If you still agree with gravity, you can stay on the ground, but don't force it on anyone else. The rest of you people who don't believe in gravity can just start floating around."

I know it's simplistic and people say, "Oh, the guy's a fool." But in about an hour I'm going to go and celebrate Mass. If reality is that that bread and wine, through my words and through the action of the Holy Spirit, become the Son of God, the Lord of the universe, then that's as real and as immutable as gravity—indeed, more so.

If that isn't reality, if our Church's teachings on salvation and life and sex aren't reality, then I need to go do something else. But I believe they are and would believe if I were the last person on Earth, because I believe and trust in God, the source and revealer of those teachings.

Think of the martyrs. Those people didn't die for a "strongly held personal religious opinion." They died because they knew what was real and it was an impossibility for them to deny it, even if it meant death. And that's the spirit of faith we need in the world today. We need people willing to die for the truth that the Church proclaims. Some may indeed shed their blood, as happens even today in parts of the world.

Many others may suffer white martyrdom: ridiculed, excluded, marginalized in their professional, academic, or social lives because they cling to the reality Christ revealed. This is the martyrdom of letting go of ourselves to follow God's will, of letting go of everything that the world has to offer us because we put the truth first.

We're not very accustomed to either kind of martyrdom here in Texas or anywhere in what used to be called the Christian West. But as with our certain death someday, it's a good spiritual discipline to prepare for martyrdom—even, perhaps, the red kind. Let us remember this and pray that, if we get there, we may have the strength to persevere.

Joseph E. Strickland is bishop of Tyler, Texas. Ordained in 1985, he was assigned to Immaculate Conception Parish in Tyler and served as parochial vicar until 1989. He was named the first vocation director for the diocese in 1987.

Strickland completed his canonical studies with a licentiate in canon law in 1994 and was reappointed as rector of the Cathedral of the Immaculate Conception in Tyler. He was appointed judicial vicar for the Diocese of Tyler in 1995, and the following year Pope John Paul II bestowed on him the title of Monsignor.

On September 29, 2012, Pope Benedict XVI appointed Msgr. Strickland the fourth bishop of Tyler.